Great Britain

6

‡‡‡‡‡‡‡‡‡‡‡‡‡‡ *National Planning Series* ‡‡‡‡‡‡‡‡‡‡‡‡‡

BERTRAM M. GROSS, GENERAL EDITOR

‡‡‡

EVERETT E. HAGEN is Professor of Economics, Massachusetts Institute of Technology, and Senior Staff member at the Center for International Studies of that institution. A member of the American Economic Association and the Royal Economic Society, he is the author of *On the Theory of Social Change* and an editor of *Planning Economic Development*.

STEPHANIE F. T. WHITE is a research associate at the Tavistock Institute of Human Relations, London, England.

†††

Great Britain

Quiet Revolution in Planning

EVERETT E. HAGEN

AND

STEPHANIE F. T. WHITE

Preface by

BERTRAM M. GROSS

SYRACUSE UNIVERSITY PRESS

First Edition 1966

ACKNOWLEDGMENT

This and other volumes in the National Planning
Series were initiated with the encouragement and
support of Stephen K. Bailey, Dean of the Maxwell Graduate School of Citizenship and Public Affairs, Syracuse University, and of his predecessor,
Harlan Cleveland. They have been made possible
through a grant from the Ford Foundation for
cross-cultural research by the Maxwell School. In
the final editing of the manuscript valuable assist-
ance was provided by Sherry Siracuse and K. M.
Shyamala Gopalan.

BERTRAM M. GROSS

Foreword

This essay, sixth in the National Planning Series conceived and fostered by Professor Bertram M. Gross, presents an account of the recent evolution of British planning institutions, and an evaluation of that evolution by a friendly outsider advised by British observers. The volume was financed by a grant to the Tavistock Institute of Human Relations from the Maxwell Graduate School of Citizenship and Public Affairs of Syracuse University, and is a product of the research program of Group A of the Tavistock Institute. It reflects the philosophy, shared by the authors and Mr. Eric Trist, director of Group A, that there is value in the joint analysis of a society by an "outsider" and an "insider"—one author detached from it and one who is a member of it. Mrs. White is a member of the Tavistock staff and Mr. Hagen is a professor of economics and of political science at the Massachusetts Institute of Technology.

Chapters I through VI and Chapter VIII were written jointly by Mr. Hagen and Mrs. White, Chapters VII and IX through XI by Mr. Hagen alone, though he would acknowledge his obligation to his coauthor for insightful and informed comments concerning drafts of those chapters. He was a guest of the Tavistock Institute during the two years 1963–65 and owes a debt of gratitude to his host, Eric Trist, inadequately expressed by its acknowledgment here.

The summary statement in Chapter I of developments during the 1950's with respect to planning is based in part on an outline set down by David Armstrong in the course of preparing a longer manuscript, still in progress, on the historical development of economic planning in Britain. The authors' debt to various informants, some of whom, as civil servants, preferred no personal acknowledgment, will appear in the text and notes.

Two special obligations, however, should be expressed here.

v

With respect to the analysis of certain aspects of British national character presented in Chapter X, Mr. Hagen would like to acknowledge his indebtedness to critical discussion of an earlier draft by Mr. Trist and Mrs. White. With respect to the same analysis and the contrast with French national characteristics and institutions, he would acknowledge his debt to the relevant chapters of Andrew Shonfield's *Modern Capitalism: The Changing Balance of Public and Private Power,* published late in 1965 by the Oxford University Press, which Mr. Shonfield permitted him to read in manuscript. Several aspects of the analysis of French planning in Chapter IX owe their development to ideas presented in Mr. Shonfield's work. Of course, none of these persons bears responsibility for the evaluation finally presented.

The text below was completed in October, 1965. As this volume goes to press, late in March, 1966, a number of further actions have been taken which are important both in themselves and as indications of the continuing evolution of the Labour government's program.

The South East Planning Board and the South East Planning Council have been established. A White Paper on the *Housing Programme, 1965 to 1970* (Cmnd. 2838) set a goal of construction of 250,000 units of public housing by 1970, and announced that subsidies would cover the excess of the interest cost of the capital for this housing above 4 per cent per year. A royal commission to recommend major changes in the structure of local government was announced. Inauguration of liner trains was again postponed, with the implication that the government not only was yielding to union resistance but also was taking a further look at the economics of the project.

Another White Paper (Cmnd. 2874) announced cash grants to subsidize industrial investment, to replace the former system of incentives via taxation allowances and accelerated depreciation. In general, the cash grants will equal 20 per cent of the investment. It is difficult to know whether the inducement to investment is increased by the change. News was also released of the government's intention to establish a financial agency to encourage selected mergers and help finance new industrial plants. The agency will be empowered to take equity ownership in any company.

A statement presented to Parliament by the Chancellor early in March summarized the economic situation and previewed the budget he would present in April. His summary of balance-of-payments figures through February showed that the speculative drain of funds from Britain during June, July, and August, 1965, was even slightly greater than estimated in Chapter XI, but that the reflux during September–February was also higher than anticipated in that chapter. The figures give ground for unease concerning whether underlying trade trends are improving significantly.

Trends in incomes and incomes policy indicate that the war for price stability is far from won. A railroad strike in February was prevented by the personal intervention of the Prime Minister. What appeared at first to be a great personal triumph for Mr. Wilson seems, on further examination, to have involved yielding more to the unions than is reassuring for the nation's incomes policy. Prices rose little from the autumn of 1965 through February, but weekly earnings of labor rose by 7 or 8 per cent. This squeeze on profits may or may not deter investment. Insofar as it squeezes fat margins it could conceivably stimulate investment. But it certainly accounts for the continuing high pressure of demand on prices. Mr. Callaghan's speech indicated that he plans no further major tax increase to counter this pressure. Present policies seem to be holding the level of output about constant; continuing increase in productivity may produce some slight slack in the economy without further fiscal restraints.

Meanwhile, Mr. Brown announced the government's intention to introduce an act requiring early notification of wage claims and some price increases—the act proposed in discussions last fall.

Altogether, the economic trends and policy announcements late in 1965 and early in 1966 give no cause for increased optimism concerning the battles for price stability, accelerated increase in productivity, and an assured surplus in the balance of payments. It is not unfair to compare the interactions of policies and events to the plot of a Shakespearean drama. We are perhaps witnessing the opening scenes of the third act, but the plot has not yet reached its climax. The expected victory of Labour in the March election is only one further incident, though an important one, in the convolution of the plot. The resolution will not begin to suggest itself for some months to come, perhaps not until 1967.

E. E. H.
S. F. T. W.

October, 1965

Contents

Foreword   v

List of Abbeviations   xiii

Boundaries and "Greatness"
A Prefatory Comment by BERTRAM M. GROSS   xv
The Bridging of National Boundaries   xvi
From "Noneconomics" to "Economics Plus"   xvii
Will Britain Be Great?   xxi

I.   The Tide Begins to Rise   1
The Status of Planning in 1960   1
Sources of Disquiet   4
Evidences of Disquiet   12

II.   New Viewpoints   14
The General Discussion   14
Incomes Policy   20
Short-Run Regulation   23
The 1961 Proposals   24

III.   Reorganization of the Control of Government Expenditures   26
The Plowden Report and Its Implementation   27

IV.   The Formation of the National Economic Development Council   33

V.   The Functioning of the National Economic Development Council   43
A Feasible Rate of Growth and the Obstacles to It   44
"Little Neddies": The Second Stage of Planning   48

VI. The National Incomes Commission 53

Formation of N.I.C. 53

Decisions by N.I.C. 55

N.E.D.C. Discusses Incomes Policy 59

VII. The Labour Government's Quiet Revolution in Planning 62

The National Plan: Numbers for 1970 63

Increasing the Pace of Advance in Productivity: Various Measures 70

Increasing the Pace of Advance in Productivity: The Department of Economic Affairs and the Economic Development Committees 76

Incomes Policy 79

VIII. Regional, Local, and Transportation Planning 89

Proposals and Actions to 1964 90

Labour Government Policies 94

Are These the Right Policies? 98

IX. Planning in France: A Frame of Reference 101

Formulating the Plan 102

Executing the Plan: "Active" Planning 105

Evaluation 110

X. British Planning and British Character 112

Differences Between French and British Planning Institutions 112

Social Origins of the Differences 114

Labour's New Institutions: Unprecedented Interference and Discrimination 124

XI. Will Planning Succeed? 129

Inflation 129

Productivity 132

The Contribution of Planning 137

The Balance of Payments: The Battle of 1964–65 143

The Balance of Payments: The War of 1966–70 152

Notes   163

Selected Bibliography   171

Index   177

TABLES

Table 1: Selected Economic Indexes, Selected Years, 1950–63   6
Table 2: Selected Economic Data, 1955–63   11
Table 3: Components of the Balance of Payments, 1953–55 and 1962–64   153
Table 4: Hypothetical Unrestricted and Restricted Balance of Payments, 1967–70   157

ABBREVIATIONS

B.N.E.C.	British National Export Council
C.B.I.	Confederation of British Industries
C.O.P.P.A.I.	Council on Prices, Productivity, and Incomes
D.E.A.	Department of Economic Affairs
E.D.C.	Economic Development Committee
F.B.I.	Federation of British Industries
N.E.D.C.	National Economic Development Council
N.E.D.O.	National Economic Development Office
N.I.C.	National Incomes Commission
N.I.E.S.R.	National Institute of Economic and Social Research
P.E.P.	Political and Economic Planning
T.U.C.	Trades Union Congress

‡‡‡

Boundaries and "Greatness"

This is the first volume in the National Planning Series that deals not with a "developing" nation but a fully industrialized one. It is most fitting, therefore, that it should discuss the country that pioneered in the process of industrializing and—from Adam Smith to John Maynard Keynes—led the world in the intellectual analysis of economic processes.

As editor of this series, I am particularly delighted with the volume as (1) an illustration of cooperative international research, (2) a successful (albeit modest) venture in the transcendence of disciplinary boundaries, and (3) a timely introduction to the question "Will Britain once again be Great?"

Many technical aspects of this study will also be of interest to national planners and students of planning. In showing the slow growth of national planning under the Macmillan government, the Hagen-White volume illustrates how national planning develops gradually rather than being created by fiat. The discussion of "incomes policy" exposes the internal contradiction (a world-wide phenomenon) created by the fact that national trade unions, the strongest political supporters of national planning, often strongly oppose the actual substance of national planning. The analysis of the interrelated roles of the Treasury, the new Ministry of Economic Affairs, and the National Economic Development Council provides a factual antidote for the dangerous nonsense that under sensible national planning arrangements all planners should be assembled under the roof of some single "central planning organ." [1] In the discussion of the revised 1964 production index, and the figures on the balance of payments, unemployment, and general growth rates,

---

[1] Many reports by United Nations experts, unfortunately, have tended to promote the fallacy of the "central planning organ." A direct rebuttal is provided in my "The Managers of National Economic Change," in Roscoe C. Martin, ed., *Public Administration and Democracy: Essays in Honor of Paul H. Appleby* (Syracuse: Syracuse University Press, 1965), pp. 101–27.

this volume provides a useful example of sophisticated skepticism in the handling of highly manipulable economic data.

Yet the three points enumerated above have much wider ramifications. Let us consider them briefly.

THE BRIDGING OF NATIONAL BOUNDARIES

Among the most fascinating aspects of national planning are the strange crosscurrents of international influence. Thus, for many decades, Russian economic planning served as a model to be followed—or fought over—in other countries. More recently, French planning has arisen as a major influence on all countries seeking "democratic" or "indicative" (rather than *dirigiste*) national planing systems.

In the spring of 1961, as Hagen and White point out, French planners crossed the Channel at the invitation of the National Institute for Economic and Social Research and "explained" their system to the British. Interest was so great that, a little later, the institute "organized a visit by a number of influential officials to France in October . . . to study French methods of planning on the spot" (p. 36). What seemed attractive in spring was no less fair in autumn, and the birth of the National Economic Development Council under the Macmillan government was accompanied by repeated assertions that by following the "French model" the British would guarantee the democratic and noncoercive nature of their new planning system.

One of the great contributions of the Hagen-White study is to suggest that the political and symbolic role of these assertions was not fully matched by their relevance to the French "facts of life." In discussing their methods with the British, the French were doing what they had done with their own countrymen—namely, emphasizing the voluntaristic participation in the formulation of general growth goals. In concentrating on the "indicative" aspects, they de-emphasized—in fact, rather strongly steered away from—the "subjunctive" and "imperative" elements in their remarkably active exploitation of direct and indirect incentives and controls (pp. 105–10). Thus the British were guided less by French reality than by their own defective perception (to which the French contributed) of French planning. Indeed, one is struck by the Hagen-

White remark that since the advent of the Labour government, with the French model no longer referred to, "for the first time in some of its aspects Britain's planning machinery is coming to resemble that in France" (p. 101). One is tempted to add that under both Macmillan and Wilson, the Dutch model, with its emphasis on business-labor agreements for wage stability, may have been more influential, although less publicly discussed.

Can any observer, rooted in his own culture, attain a non-culture-bound view of these complex currents? It is highly doubtful; the best one can do is try. And the best way of trying is to join with people in other cultures in a mutual effort of checking and cross-checking. In more ways than meet the eye, the Hagen-White volume is a product of such international collaboration. The most obvious is joint authorship by an American economics professor and a British sociologist. In addition, there has been the sustained cooperation between the two sponsoring institutions, the Maxwell School and the Tavistock Institute of Human Relations. Beyond this, a major contributor to the thinking revealed in the book was Michel Crozier, France's outstanding sociologist, whose *The Bureaucratic Phenomenon* provides a path-breaking analysis of national character in different countries.[2] Crozier's preliminary materials on French planning (for a book in preparation as a part of this series) were of invaluable service to Professor Hagen and Mrs. White. Reciprocal benefits are provided by the fact that Professor Hagen has not only helped the British see Britain in perspective but has made a distinct contribution (aided valiantly by Andrew Shonfield) to French efforts to understand themselves. One might hope that in the not too distant future a Frenchman and an Englishman might collaborate with an American in the extremely difficult task of understanding guided economic and social change under President Johnson's plans for a "Great Society."

FROM "NONECONOMICS" TO "ECONOMICS PLUS"

With the slow maturation of modern social science, more and more people are coming to realize that economic growth cannot

[2] Chicago: Univ. of Chicago Press, 1964. In this book Crozier analyzes a French "clerical agency" and an "industrial monopoly" and uses his findings concerning bureaucratic organization as a path toward a better understanding of French culture and the differences between it and the cultures of other societies.

be understood by economic analysis alone or successfully pursued by economic measures alone.

The first and easiest stage of this realization comes with the discovery or uncovering of noneconomic variables. Everett Hagen's earlier work, *On the Theory of Social Change: How Economic Growth Begins,* made a memorable contribution to this stage.[3] "The initial approach of economists, in the surge of interest after World War II in the problems of growth of low-income economies," he pointed out, "was to assume that any barriers to growth that might exist are economic ones, and that the process of economic growth is adequately dealt with by economic analysis alone." He also noted that most theories dealing with economic barriers to growth "assume that the central problem in growth is capital formation, and . . . that sufficient technological creativity to carry forward economic growth is present in all societies." [4] In contrast to these single-factor theories, Hagen asserted that "a model that explains economic growth must take into account non-economic as well as economic aspects of human behavior. . . . In the countries in which the transition to economic growth has occurred it has been concomitant with far-reaching change in political organization, social structure, and attitudes toward life." [5] Illustrating this thesis by historical examinations of various countries, he had this to say about Britain:

> In Britain the Industrial Revolution which gathered force gradually in the eighteenth century followed some centuries of social and religious tensions. Willingness to be ruled by a king and a small select group of nobles was replaced by a growing sense that such rule was wrong, and through their representatives in Parliament successive generations of towns-people progressively destroyed the hierarchy of political power. It culminated in the adoption of Calvinism by the Scots and the emergence of strong Protestant dissent among the townsmen of England. And the Dissenters and lowland Scots were present among the economic innovators in numbers

[3] Homewood, Illinois: Dorsey Press, 1962. Although published in 1962, the ideas in this book began to influence others by the time Hagen started formal work on it in 1956.
[4] *Ibid.,* pp. 36–49.
[5] *Ibid.,* pp. 25–26.

out of all proportion to their numbers in the population at large.[6]

He then went on to analyze a cluster of noneconomic variables that lifted many eyebrows among his fellow economists: childhood upbringing, the revolt against arbitrary fathers, and the inner tensions felt by minority groups. Above all, he maintained that innovating personalities with needs, values, and conditions conducive to technological creativity come into being only when the members of some social group feel "that their purposes and values in life are not respected by groups in society whom they respect and whose esteem they value." [7]

In calling attention to these cultural and personality variables, Hagen made no pretense of providing a *complete* explanation of economic growth. Indeed, his task of identifying previously neglected noneconomic variables could hardly have been carried out so brilliantly if he had also taken on the more complex task of relating them to the variables traditionally handled by economists. Thus his earlier analysis of culture and personality can scarcely be expected to yield any judgments as to the best growth policies to be followed by either the British or the Burmese.

A more significant stage in the analysis of economic change comes when social scientists move still further and, having become accustomed to handling noneconomic variables, move from "noneconomics" to "economics plus." This is the stage in which the economic and noneconomic variables are brought together at a higher level of integration. In their discussion of "British Planning and British Character" (Chapter X) Hagen and White reach this level. They discuss the differences between French and British planning in terms of deep-rooted social values and traditions. But instead of assuming that these values and traditions are unchangeable, they deal directly with the kinds of decisions that may be taken in order to create new attitudes and, indeed, promote major changes in "British character" (pp. 124–28).

In this connection, it is interesting to note that in such a stiff and staid document as the British Plan for 1965–70 frequent mention is made of the need to change attitudes affecting pro-

[6] *Ibid.*, p. 26. See also Chapter 13, "England: Continental Values and Anglo-Saxon Virtues."
[7] *Ibid.*, p. 185.

ductivity, innovation, and dynamism. In September 1965, one may safely infer, it was politically feasible to publish documents on the need for attitude changes; this was hardly the case five years earlier. As a result (although perhaps unanticipated by the planners), we now find the government constructively criticized for not specifying just how attitudes may be changed. Indeed, independently of Hagen and White, an Oxford economist has taken up this theme and—without absolving the government—pointed the finger of blame at social scientists as a group:

> This particular gap in the plan is partly due to the fact that we know very little about how to operate on people's attitudes. The gaps in our knowledge of the relevant economic variables, to which I have already made reference above, are serious enough, but the gaps in our understanding of the determinants of, say, managerial attitudes to research or technological progress, or of employees' attitudes to innovation, are much greater. Sociologists are quite ready to concede, I believe, that their subject is at an even more rudimentary stage than is economics, and many of the aspects of attitudes that I have been referring to concern the sociologist much more than the economist.[8]

By stimulating additional critiques of this type, the Hagen-White analysis will undoubtedly promote more effective demand for multidisciplinary analyses that go still further in making the great leap forward to "economics plus." As this demand grows, the Tavistock Institute of Human Relations—with its unique combination of an interdisciplinary and clinical approach to the problems of nations and regions as well as organizations and individuals—has a major role to play. This role is heralded by the appointment of Wilfred Brown, whose famous reorganization of the Glacier Metals, Ltd., was undertaken with the help of Tavistock advisers,[9] as Joint

---

[8] W. Beckerman (Balliol College, Oxford), "Economic Planning and Data Requirements," unpublished paper presented to the Royal Statistical Society, 1965 (mimeo).

[9] Wilfred Brown, *Exploration in Management* (London: Heinemann, 1960). An equally significant example of Tavistock's capacity to contribute to real-life solutions of economic and social problems is provided in the classic study—referred to briefly by Hagen and White (p. 168)—E. L. Trist, G. W. Higgin, W. Murray, and A. B. Pollock, *Organizational Choice: Capabilities of Groups at the Coal Face under Changing Technologies* (London: Tavistock Publications, 1963).

Minister of State in the Board of Trade (p. 160). Other countries could benefit immeasurably by the building of similar institutions.

WILL BRITAIN BE GREAT?

Some years ago, when Eric Trist and I first made the plans leading to the Hagen-White study, I bolstered up my courage and asked a minor editorial question that had been bothering me for a long time.

"What shall we call your country?" I asked. "Shall we say 'United Kingdom' (which is the way you appear on the official roll-call of the United Nations) or 'England' or 'Great Britain'? "

Trist pondered a moment and, with an almost imperceptible trace of painful modesty, answered, "No, not Great, just Britain." Behind his words I sensed the anguish of thousands of thoughtful Britains pondering on the decline of the Empire and of glories never to return. And so his country appeared as simply 'Britain' in all the earlier lists of our planning studies—*until* suddenly one day there appeared in our offices the final title of this volume with the proudly affirmed words: *Great* Britain.

The reason for this change to titular greatness, I am convinced, was neither the *noblesse oblige* of Professor Hagen nor the patriotism of Mrs. White. Rather, something had happened in the interval: namely, *the decision to effect a quiet revolution in Britain's national planning for economic growth*. This decision, in my judgment, reflected a deep-seated and widespread aspiration for a return to greatness in the world.

In Montesquieu's *The Spirit of Laws* there is a famous passage that might be pondered by all national elites aspiring to greatness:

> Though all governments have the same general end, which is that of preservation, yet each has another particular object. Increase of dominion was the object of Rome; war, that of Sparta; religion, that of the Jewish laws; commerce, that of Marseilles; public tranquillity, that of the laws of China; navigation, that of the laws of Rhodes; natural liberty, that of the policy of the savages; in general, the pleasures of the prince, that of the despotic states; that of monarchies, the prince's and the kingdom's glory.

Recently, a brilliant historian, Frank Manuel of New York University, has extended this analysis by pointing out that in the past, "Great societies have been praised for their military prowess, lawful orderliness and security, devotion to beauty, absolute commitment to a principle of religious transcendence, the prevalence of warm communal feeling, their size, power, and grandeur, their opportunities for sensate or spiritual happiness, their harmony and justice, peacefulness, egalitarianism, freedom, duration in time, constancy and changelessness, their pursuit of excellence." [10] Today, we need a modern Montesquieu who will enrich this analysis by applying such concepts to the latent purposes of such commanding world figures as Charles de Gaulle, Lyndon B. Johnson, and Mao Tse Tung and of the elites that surround and support them.

In the meantime three propositions are becoming increasingly clear—although their acceptability seems to vary in inverse ratio to their significance.

First, in the modern world economic growth seems to be a necessary precondition for *any* kind of greatness. Although nations and regimes vary considerably in their capacity to do anything about it, this point is generally accepted. In Britain it has become a basic political axiom.

Second, and more important, economic growth is not readily achieved if it is the only aim pursued. Man does not live by bread —or affluence—alone. High economic growth rates require motivations to achieve noneconomic ends—social justice, the restoration of national dignity, military might, culture, and beauty—that can be achieved only through expanded economic means. It is interesting to note that the bold economic growth targets set forth by the late President Kennedy in the United States did not become realities until after his successor's program for a "Great Society" had shifted the emphasis from the quantity of goods to the quality of life. In reviewing the British plan and particularly the 1966 political campaign in Britain, one is struck by the dull grayness of the steady pounding upon cold economic variables. It is not hard to understand why the electoral turnout declined. It is harder to

[10] "The Great Societies: Past and Future," paper presented at the Arthur F. Bentley Seminar on the Great Society, Maxwell Graduate School of Citizenship and Public Affairs, Syracuse University, March 25, 1966. To be published in Bertram M. Gross, ed., *The Great Society: Search and Appraisal* (New York: Basic Books).

understand why British leaders have taken so long to learn from the domestic political examples set by both Lyndon B. Johnson and Charles de Gaulle. In any case, this was probably the last British political campaign to be fought with economic slogans alone. From here on we may expect that—with direct implications for economic expansion—British politics will be characterized by "economics plus."

Third, and even more important, is the fact that military power is an increasingly dubious form of greatness. The vast, unused, nuclear stockpiles of American and Russian "overkill" are symbols of nationalized madness, potential instruments for destroying mankind and, with it, all human power for good or evil. The new nonnuclear weapon systems—used unsuccessfully so far in Viet Nam, Laos, and Cambodia against ill-equipped guerilla fighters—have made the United States look ugly and foolish, not great, in the eyes of the world. The overextension of military commitments abroad has—at least temporarily—reduced President Johnson's vision of a Great Society in America to what Senator Fulbright has called an "empty dream." In a major address at the University of Connecticut, the Chairman of the Senate Foreign Relations Committee made this double-edged comment:

> There is a kind of madness in the facile assumption that we can raise the many billions of dollars necessary to rebuild our schools and cities and public transport and eliminate the pollution of air and water while also spending tens of billions to finance an "open-ended" war in Asia. . . .
>
> But even if the material resources can somehow be drawn from an expanding economy, I do not think that the spiritual resources will long be forthcoming from an angry and disappointed people.[11]

With these soberly pessimistic words, Senator Fulbright knew that he was commenting on the efforts of Lyndon B. Johnson—his old friend and former colleague on the floor of the Senate—to attain a place in history as a Great President beside the greatest Western leader of this century, Franklin D. Roosevelt.

In the same spirit, one might venture a similar comment on the future of Harold Wilson's efforts to regain greatness for Britain.

[11] *New York Times*, March 22, 1966.

Out of power, Wilson and the Labour Party called for a cutting down on military commitments derived from the remnants of imperial glory. Fresh in power, they cut. But soon afterwards—in responding both to the actions of De Gaulle and the direct pressures of the Johnson administration—they once again returned to quasi-imperialist dreams of military power and "international responsibilities" east of Suez. Indeed, as Hagen and White point out, "the deterioration of Britain's balance of payments from the 1950's to the 1960's is not due to a worsening of the trade position (nor to an increase in net private long-term investment abroad). The increasing trade deficit . . . has not appeared" (pp. 152–154). Moreover, "the severity of the balance-of-payments crisis of 1964–65 is due largely to the fact that other components of the balance of payments had not improved sufficiently to offset the increased governmental expenditures abroad required by the international responsibilities of Britain" (p. 155). Although these "international responsibilities" are not specifically mentioned, it is clear that the reference is mainly (not entirely) to Britain's effort to maintain its second-class membership in the "nuclear club." Also, one is left to speculate how Britain balances off the foreign exchange gains from American-sponsored actions to support the British pound against the foreign exchange costs of British action in support of American foreign policy. In any case—to paraphrase Senator Fulbright—it is highly doubtful whether Britain can raise the billions needed to modernize her society while spending many billions competing with De Gaulle for military grandeur. But even if the material resources can somehow be drawn from a more modernized economy, I do not think that the spiritual resources will long be coming from the new generation of Britons born in an island without empire.

"The great society, while finding true elements of greatness in Johnsonian America," Manuel has written, "is still rather burdened with heroic conceptions that are as antiquated as Achilles. We act as though every insult must be requited a thousandfold. Talk of destiny or mission or honor in the tradition of the duello still seems to dominate polity. Such notions belonged to other great societies; they have no place in ours. . . . The age of heroes, like the age of the gods, is dead. It is time that the age of men began." [12]

[12] "The Great Societies: Past and Future."

In Britain the age of Churchill—like that of Palmerston, Rhodes, Gladstone, and Disraeli—is dead. There shall be no more dominion by "the prince's and the kingdom's glory," no more *pukka sahib* drinking gin and tonic served by the natives, and probably no new supersonic transports and intercontinental missiles ready to support the British in any role as a world model, missionary or crusader. The greatness of any future Britain is not foreshadowed by the broken shards of empire. It is heralded by the incomparable *dramatis personae* that includes, among many others, the names of Shakespeare, Milton, Shelley, Darwin, Florence Nightingale, Shaw, Rutherford and—let us not forget—Smith, Marshall, and Keynes. Should leaders like Harold Wilson be able to remember the true elements of human glory in Britain's past, then Britain would, perhaps, become truly great.

BERTRAM . M. GROSS

Syracuse, New York
Spring 1966

The Tide Begins to Rise

THE STATUS OF PLANNING IN 1960

The year 1960 is a convenient rather than a precise date by which to mark the reversal of the postwar tide against economic planning in Britain. The turn of the tide had perhaps occurred earlier, say in 1957 or 1958. But in 1960 it was indisputably certain that the waters were advancing, not still receding, and we shall use that date as our starting point.

In referring to economic planning we shall have in mind governmental action to influence the pace and direction of economic movement: not merely the setting of economic goals, which may be only a formal framework, but the designing of economic controls and stimuli.

The 1948 "long-term plan" whose formulation had been a condition of the receipt of economic aid under the Marshall Plan had been forgotten by 1960. The Central Economic Planning staff which had been formed by Sir Stafford Cripps in 1947 had long since gradually been converted into two subordinate units of the Treasury concerned in a vague way with natural resources. The Economic Planning Board formed by him in 1948 to bring Treasury officials and selected industrialists together in national planning still met at intervals, but its function had vanished.

"Administrative" or "physical" controls, adopted comprehensively during the war, and once considered by Labour party theoreticians as essential tools of economic control in peacetime also, had been abandoned. The process of abandonment had been in-

1

itiated by the postwar Labour government. The massive rearmament program launched in 1950, when the Korean War caused alarm, had delayed the removal of some controls and caused the reinstatement of some others; but before that program the Labour government had dismantled most controls over materials distribution and some consumer rationing. After the hump of production for rearmament had passed, the Conservative government which gained power in 1951 on a pledge to "set the people free" accelerated the process. The only important direct controls remaining by the end of 1954 were coal rationing and quantitative restrictions on some imports (mainly dollar imports).

Until 1955, although many foreign exchange controls had been relaxed, two types of "abnormal" controls were still used when necessary to meet short-run crises in the balance of payments: the exchange rate for current payments was permitted to fluctuate, and imports were reduced by administrative controls. Early in 1955 the Bank of England moved one step further toward "normal foreign trade" by beginning support of the "transferable sterling" rate. This step largely freed British importers and foreign suppliers from the risk of loss through exchange fluctuation. In April the government took a final step. In his budget speech the Chancellor of the Exchequer explicitly rejected the tightening of quantitative import restrictions to meet the balance-of-payments crisis which was threatening. It was clear that thereafter the tools to be used were the "conventional" ones: increase in the Bank Rate to attract short-term capital and credit restriction plus fiscal measures to restrict aggregate production in Britain and thus the demand for imports. In 1958 the remaining quantitative controls on imports, as well as coal rationing, were ended. The battery of measures which had been thought of as planning measures was thus reduced essentially to fiscal adjustments and monetary regulation to meet the successive problems of the short run.

The use of fiscal measures as one instrument for this purpose was the one important control introduced during the war which was retained. Keynesian theory had come to govern the use of these monetary-fiscal tools by the Labour government before it lost power, and the Conservative government of 1951 accepted the theory. There was objection to some of the implications of Keynesian theory by pre-Keynesians in the Conservative party who thought it unsound, and at the other extreme by advocates of direct controls in the Labour party who thought it inadequate. The *Economist* saw fit by the use of the term Butskellism to identify these tools (and other measures) with Gaitskell and Butler rather than to treat them as doctrine fully accepted in either party. However, it was clear that no future government would reject either Keynesian theory or the central use of fiscal and monetary measures to regulate trends in production, employment, and perhaps prices, and in imports and the balance of payments.[1] The Conservatives termed the use of these tools not planning but the regulation of a free economy, and the Labour party members in whose view only physical controls constituted planning agreed with this description.

The two parties came to disagree rather basically on an important issue in the application of these fiscal and monetary tools. R. A. Butler, chancellor from the formation of a Conservative government in October, 1951, until December, 1955, and Harold Macmillan, chancellor from that time until January, 1957, were both "expansionists." But gradually between 1955 and 1957 the relative emphasis on protection of the pound, if there seemed to be a choice between that and economic expansion, increased in the minds of some government leaders. In September, 1957, the then chancellor, Mr. Thorneycroft, could say in a formal speech to an annual meeting of the International Monetary Fund that credit restriction and limitation of public investment would be pushed to whatever lengths necessary to prevent inflation and protect the pound. "If inflationary pressures grow inside the economy, other things may alter, other aspects of policy may have to be adjusted, but the strain will not be placed on the value of the pound sterling." [2] The implications seemed clear that the "other things" might include production and employment.

Mr. Thorneycroft had urged deflation to a politically unpalatable point. He was replaced as chancellor in January, 1958. But his successor, Mr. Heathcoat Amory, urged and applied a policy whose general tenor was the same. The Labour party, on the other hand, maintained that the instruments used to preserve international financial stability must not be ones which interfered with the maintenance of full employment at home. In practice this meant that in the event of a foreign exchange crisis they would have restricted imports by quantitative controls rather than by reducing the level of demand for imports by reducing the level of domestic economic activity.

The issue, it should be noted, was not over the importance of maintaining the exchange rate. Although the exchange rate may have been more sacred to the Conservatives than to the Labour party, both parties accepted without question its importance. The issue was Labour party emphasis on the maintenance of maximum employment even in the short run versus Conservative party stress on a free market for imports. Even here the difference between the two parties was not an extreme one. While the Conservatives were more willing then Labour to allow employment to sag, as an alternative to controls over imports, they were not willing to allow it to sag very far. Neither party was ready to tolerate a percentage of unemployment which both major parties in the United States had accepted throughout the last six years of the 1950's.[3]

The nation as a whole was committed to several economic goals, and these in turn were regarded as means to the end of maximum human welfare. The economic goals were full employment, price stability, rejection of price controls to achieve it, accelerated economic growth, and maintenance of equilibrium in the balance of payments without further devaluation of the pound. Whether these five goals were compatible was not considered; the nation was committed to all. Even though the Labour party gave lip service to "controls" as an instrument in planning, the main wing of the party joined the Conservative and Liberal parties in rejecting price controls. There was a wide consensus that the use of price controls would deter economic growth and that the interferences with economic freedom which price controls constitute is evil in itself. Only a left-wing group within the Labour party— fairly large and intense in its belief—dissented.

SOURCES OF DISQUIET

In 1960 and 1961 a movement for the establishment of new institutions for economic planning gained force. A tide of disquiet affected the nation as a whole, and carried both parties with it. The parties came to agree that certain minimum institutions were essential, even though important differences in the nature and scope of planning emerged in the debate which took place.

Basically, all of the currents of unease felt by the nation stemmed from a deeply felt sense that the performance of the economy and its institutions was inadequate. During the preceding decade not one of the economic goals had been realized to the degree desired.

One of the specific sources of disquiet was that the rate of increase in production and income in Britain, both in the aggregate and per capita, was markedly less than in the economies of Western Europe. The performance of the American economy also seemed much better than that of Britain, but this was in the main an illusion. It was the labor force of the United States, not its output per worker, that was growing much faster. Actually, Britain's performance had not deteriorated. Her rate of increase in output per worker, just under 2 per cent per year, was entirely respectable—indeed, rather rapid—by Western historical standards. But Western European countries, blasted out of their ruts by the war, had responded by an unprecedented acceleration of advance in productivity and Britain had not, and as a consequence British leaders felt inadequate, or guilty, or both.

Second, there was uneasiness at continuing price rises that threatened Britain's ability to compete in world markets and at the failure of existing institutions to cope with them. The data presented in Table 1 provide more than ample justification for this alarm. From 1953 (when postwar reconstruction may be regarded as complete) to 1960, export prices of manufactured goods fell by 17 per cent in Italy and by 1 per cent in France, and remained constant in West Germany. They rose by 12 per cent in Britain. Only in the United States did the rise exceed that in Britain.[4]

Moreover, the change in competitive position relative to the continent was not fully reflected in the price indexes. The more rapid technical advance on the continent included the introduction of new products and improvements in the design of products not reflected in the price indexes but reflected in the gradual displacement of British goods from some markets.

Britain's prices were rising year after year because of the annual demands of her trade unions for wage increases much in excess of those in productivity, and the accession to these demands year after year by employers. For labor as a whole the wage demands were futile. The purchasing power of workers increased by no more than if wages had risen by several per cent per year less and prices had remained stable. Perhaps, quite apart from the economic effects, uneasiness was created by a sense of an inexorable and irrational trend pushing the nation towards disaster.

As a result of the price increases and relatively slow product

TABLE 1

SELECTED ECONOMIC INDEXES, SELECTED YEARS, 1950–63

(1953 = 100)

A. Hourly Earnings in Manufacturing

	U.S.A.	U.K.	W. Germany *	France †	Italy
1950	83	81	78	—	85
1953	100	100	100	100	100
1958	120	137	139	159	128
1959	125	143	146	168	131
1960	129	155	158	183	137
1961	133	164	175	197	147
1962	136	171	194	214	169
1963	141	178	208	232	199

B. Output per Hour in Manufacturing (Seasonally adjusted) ‡

	U.S.A.	U.K.	W. Germany *	France †	Italy
1950	93	97	85	—	—
1953	100	100	100	100	
1958	114	110	123	141	104
1959	120	115	119	146	109
1960	124	121	140	155	119
1961	128	121	144	161	127
1962	134	124	151	168	140
1963	139	131	158	175	150

C. Volume of Exports

	U.S.A.	U.K.	W. Germany *	France †	Italy
1950	92	106	57	96	93
1953	100	100	100	100	100
1958	127	116	196	139	164
1959	127	120	220	167	201
1960	151	127	251	194	243
1961	152	129	267	206	289
1962	160	131	275	208	320
1963	168	137	306	225	339

D. Export Prices of Manufactures

	U.S.A.	U.K.	W. Germany *	France †	Italy
1951	99	98	99	92	105
1953	100	100	100	100	100
1958	112	110	100	102	86
1959	116	110	100	94	80
1960	118	112	102	99	83
1961	119	113	107	99	79
1962	119	115	108	99	78
1963	119	118	107	100	81

E. Cost of Living

	U.S.A.	U.K.	W. Germany *	France †	Italy
1950	89	81	82	77	86
1953	100	100	100	100	100
1958	108	119	110	120	114
1959	109	120	111	129	114
1960	110	120	112	139	116
1961	111	124	115	152	118
1962	113	130	119	165	124
1963	114	133	122	180	133

* All industries.

† Manufacturing, construction, transport, and distribution.

‡ 1953 data are not available for Italy. To present an index roughly comparable with those for other countries, it has been *assumed* that output per manhour in manufacturing in 1953 was 4 per cent below that in 1958. This is pure assumption and only the differentials among later years have quantitative significance.

Sources: For A and B, N.I.E.S.R. *Economic Review,* August, 1962, and November, 1964; for D, *ibid.,* February, 1963, and November, 1964; for C and E, I.M.F. *International Financial Statistics,* August, 1959, and December, 1964. Figures for 1950 have been converted from 1950 = 100.

improvement, although rising world income and demand caused Britain's exports to rise, they rose only sluggishly. From 1953 to 1958, while the average annual rate of increase in the physical volume of exports of the United States was 5 per cent, that of France 7 per cent, of Italy 10, and of West Germany 14, that of Britain was only 3 per cent. The increase in the disparity between 1958 and 1960 was even more alarming. Converting the figures again to an annual basis, for easier comparison with the 1953–58 period, the annual percentage increases were: Britain, 4 per cent; United States, 9; West Germany, 13; France 18; Italy, 22. And even the 1 per cent acceleration in Britain's increase in exports was a short-run phenomenon, not maintained.

If these increases in Britain's exports had represented net improvements in her balance-of-payments position, there would have been no foreign exchange problem. However, as her production rose, her volume of imports rose faster than that of her exports. Because export prices were rising, the value of exports nevertheless rose faster than that of imports, but not enough faster to offset Britain's other expenditures abroad and increase her monetary reserves. These remained precariously low. In 1955, as her economy moved from a condition of slight slack to tight full employment, her imports rose, her payments materially exceeded her receipts, and a run on sterling resulted. Confidence was restored by restrictive fiscal and monetary measures, but no one knew when the crisis might recur. This threat was a third source of alarm.

If Britain was to retain her position as international banker, she needed to *increase* her monetary reserves. For world trade was continually increasing, and required a continually increasing supply of funds to finance it. Britain's position relative to the Western European countries needed to be improved, whereas in fact it was steadily deteriorating. The sense of a task to be performed, in which Britain was failing, was therefore all the more oppressive.

Concern about Britain's international economic position was increased by the formation of the European Common Market. In the years from 1957 to 1960, as the economic integration of the Six proceeded even more rapidly than scheduled, British leaders were afraid lest the erection of this large free-trade area from which Britain was excluded by a tariff wall would materially worsen Britain's always precarious balance of payments. However, in view of the relatively slow rate of increase in British productivity, they were equally worried that if she did apply for entrance and was admitted, her balance of payments would also deteriorate. The Chancellor's announcement on July 25, 1961, that a National Economic Development Council would be formed was made in the knowledge that Great Britain was about to apply for admission to the Common Market, and her application was pending throughout the entire period of formation of N.E.D.C. It may be inferred that the government was spurred to immediate action concerning N.E.D.C. by its decision to apply for membership in the European Common Market.

An accelerated rate of advance in productivity and thereby of economic growth was deemed necessary not only to meet these crucially important problems but for an additional reason: to make possible an expanded public program of social welfare without too great a diminution of the rate of increase in private income and expenditure. Moreover, it was thought that a more rapid rate of advance in productivity would help to solve the problem of rising prices, for it would make possible higher wage increases than otherwise without price increases. These two problems interlocked, for it was anticipated that if expanded programs of social welfare had to be financed by appreciable increases in tax rates, trade unions would demand correspondingly enlarged wage increases.

Third, the British were disquieted by the results of the economic control policies followed during the 1950's, especially after the removal of direct controls. As a balance-of-payments crisis threatened in 1955, credit restrictions were instituted (rise in Bank Rate, restrictions on hire-purchase, directions to commercial banks to reduce the aggregate volume of their advances), then certain taxes were increased, and early in 1956 credit restrictions were increased further and public investment reduced. In September, 1957, the same measures were tightened further, the Bank Rate being increased to 7 per cent.

When unemployment increased by mid-1958 to levels higher than any known since the war, between July and the end of the year, each of these measures except tax increases was reversed. The ceiling on the bank advances, restrictions on capital issues, and restrictions on hire-purchase were removed; the Bank Rate was reduced progressively to 4 per cent, and public investment programs were increased. Then in the April 1959 budget, large cuts were made in tax rates. (Taxes are normally altered only at budget time in April.)

As a result, the year 1959 showed the fastest increase in industrial production since the war. But 1960 brought a trade deficit equaled only in 1955, and the largest balance-of-payments deficit of the decade. So the various measures for credit squeeze were again applied, and in the April 1961 budget the Chancellor asked for and obtained permission to alter all consumer taxes by 10 per cent in either direction between budgets and to impose a surcharge on employer's National Insurance contributions. In July he used the first of these powers.

There were widespread protests that these Stop-Go tactics inhibited economic growth by preventing rational investment planning by industrial concerns. The hearings of the Committee on the Working of the Monetary System (the Radcliffe Committee) provided a forum for many such protests in 1957 and 1958, and such objections were registered in a moderate degree by that committee in 1959 [5] and more forcefully in the publications of the National Institute of Economic and Social Research and the Federation of British Industries.

One basis for the protests was the fact that, because of Stop-Go, interest rates might rise just as a company was planning to raise money for investment. The large variations in Bank Rate and the accompanying controls over bank loans affected not only short-term rates but also long-term rates and the availability of credit at any rate (since banks practiced rationing rather than boosting their rates to the maximum the market would bear). The erratic nature of these changes must have been extremely disturbing to the planning of the financing of investment to any companies who had insufficient internal funds for the purpose.

However, the objections went beyond this. Stop-Go interfered with investment planning, it was said, because it interfered with forecasts of future demand for one's products. Actually, considered from year to year, the fluctuations in the upward trend of demand for industrial or other products caused by Stop-Go were not great. The annual data of Table 2 indicate that annual fluctuations in neither total nor industrial production were large enough to be the source of great difficulty in planning investment. Only from 1957 to 1958 did the volume of industrial production turn down, and the variations in the annual data between 1955 and 1963 from those of a smooth curve connecting the two dates are not enough to have disturbed greatly the advance of increases in capacity. The monthly data, for example those of 1958 and 1959, of course show greater variations. Such short-lived fluctuations should not greatly impede investment planning, if the planners can count with certainty on the longer-run course of demand. The fluctuations in the demand for consumer durable goods, caused by regulation of hire-purchase, were no doubt great enough at times seriously to affect production in the industries affected, and the demand for machine tools and construction also underwent greater fluctuations than demand in general. Even in machine tools and construction, however, if the fluctuations interfered with the planning of technical advances, this must have been due at least as much to lack of faith in the continuing long-run expansion of demand as to the short-run fluctuations.

TABLE 2

SELECTED ECONOMIC DATA, 1955–63

(Cols. 1–6—Indexes: 1955 = 100)

Year	1 G.D.P., Constant Prices *	2 G.D.P., in Constant Prices (per person engaged) *	3 Wage Rates, Manufac- turing	4 Price of Manufac- tured Products	5 Unit Values of Exports	6 Industrial Production	7 Unemploy- ment (per cent of employees)
1955	100	100	100	100	100	100	1.08
6	101	100	107	104	103	100	1.19
7	103	102	113	108	109	102	1.43
8	103	103	116	109	108	101	2.10
9	107	107	120	109	106	106	2.17
60	113	111	122	111	109	113	1.62
61	115	112	127	113	109	114	1.52
2	116	113	131	114	110	116	2.03
3	121	118	135	117	113	120	2.50

* Between 1955 and 1963 the civilian labor force increased by 5 per cent. The data of columns 1 and 2, which imply an increase of only some 3 per cent, are therefore inconsistent.

Source: N.I.E.S.R. *Economic Review,* November, 1964. Converted from 1958 = 100.

Stop-Go was accused of checking growth in productivity in a more subtle way. By frustrating expectations of a rapid rise in demand, it was argued, Stop-Go deterred companies from taking measures to increase their output per worker to meet the demand. The scope of this argument is limited, for most technical advances are introduced to reduce the cost per unit of output, or to improve the product, whether or not demand is expanding. However, quite apart from this fact, it is difficult to see a valid argument here other than the one discussed in the preceding paragraph. The basic determinant of the rate of increase in the demand for the products of any industry is the rate of increase in the country's productive capacity and income at full employment. The argument must be that, in the absence of Stop-Go, the fictitious expectation that a boom could continue beyond the economy's capacity would have so simulated technical advance that capacity would very rapidly have been increased and the fiction would have become reality. There was very little basis for this version of pulling oneself up by one's bootstraps; it was mainly a comforting sort of self-deception. That productivity should be rising so much faster in continental countries than in Britain must have created a considerable sense of guilt, and it was reassuring to find some governmental policy to which the blame could be attributed. It is also possible that a sense of frustration, and even humilation, at the sight of one's government so incapable of meeting successive contingencies smoothly that its policies bounced about erratically, may have provided an emotional basis for the outcries.

At any rate, in business, academic, and labor circles demands arose for measures which would obviate the necessity of Stop-Go.

Other factors also contributed to the disquiet. One was the perception that the existing machinery for economic analysis was inadequate, so that not all of the effects of various Stop-Go measures were accurately foreseen when the measures were taken. Another was that no adequate machinery for the integral analysis and control of public expenditures existed. Longer-run historical trends also may slowly have been pressing Britain toward increased governmental intervention in the economic processes. But the conditions summarized here were the immediate causes of the uneasiness at the end of the 1950's which gave rise to a new concern with planning public expenditure and a new interest in the performance of the economy.

Evidences of Disquiet

A series of governmental and private actions during the last three years of the 1950's gave evidence of this new concern. In 1957 the Committee on the Working of the Monetary System (the

Radcliffe Committee) was appointed and the Council on Prices, Productivity, and Incomes (C.O.P.P.A.I.) was created by the government. In the same year the private research organization known as Political and Economic Planning (P.E.P.) began a study of economic growth in Britain, and in 1958 the Federation of British Industries (F.B.I.) began to publish its *Survey into Industrial Trends.* In 1958 also the Select Committee on Estimates of the House of Commons prepared a report highly critical of the Treasury machinery for the control of public expenditure. In 1959 the government set up a Committee on the Control of Public Expenditure (the Plowden Committee). In the same year the National Institute of Economic and Social Research (N.I.E.S.R.), an autonomous and influential economic research organization, began to publish its *Economic Review.* In the spring of 1960 the government appointed a special advisory group of the British Transport Commission to examine the structure, finance, and working of the organizations controlled by the Commission. Later in the same year a government White Paper on *Public Investment in Britain* (Cmnd. 1203) was published.

These governmental actions are all discussed further in the chapters which follow. They were more or less *ad hoc* actions dealing with separate though important aspects of the economic problem. By about 1960 support began to form for a more integrated attack of some sort on the problem as a whole. Choice among the various economic goals was not contemplated. Rather, new institutions were sought by which the inconsistencies among the goals could be eliminated so that all might be attained.

II

New Viewpoints

THE GENERAL DISCUSSION

The 1959 Trades Union Congress (T.U.C.) *Report* had set forth
the T.U.C. conviction of the necessity for government commitment
to and government policy for growth. "Support for the objective of
full employment and higher living standards essentially involves
support for policies of economic growth and expansion. . . . Continuing expansion will not happen of its own accord." Alan Birch,
general secretary of the Shop, Distributive, and Allied Trades Union
and a leader in an attempt within the unions to reconcile union and
national goals, continued this theme in an article in *The Director*
for October, 1959. "The more successful this policy is in ensuring
a continuous rise in output, the less likelihood there is of the collective bargaining machinery being unable to cope with wage movements to the satisfaction of trade unionists without a wages and
prices spiral." An article in the May, 1960, issue of the T.U.C.
publication *Labour* developed another aspect of the theme. "There
is no clear indication that the Government have any clear long-term
view of the country's needs; on the contrary, their concern seems
to be almost entirely with the short-term balance of the economy.
. . . Our economic growth still remains largely undirected, and
there is no evidence that the government have any clear policy for
the industrial development of Britain which is a necessary contribution to the solution of the difficulties facing us in Europe."

These statements surprised no one, for planning had long been
a program of the unions and the Labour party. The new development was a growing commitment to planning within the Conserva-

tive party. However, this does not mean that the Conservatives had swung around to the Labour view. Earlier, "planning" had been used exclusively to mean the establishment of a "command economy" in which the volume of production, at least in industries determined to be basic, and the use of the products of these industries, would be determined by administrative decision rather than by the market. The doctrine being emphasized in about 1960 was one of regulating the conditions of the market so that the market would guide producers to desired ends. Such regulation was the sort of planning which Conservative party leaders were beginning increasingly to endorse. However, in endorsing it they were also coming to accept the desirability of forming a body or bodies to scrutinize the behavior of the private economy and recommend policies to influence economic trends—a procedure they had previously felt to be somewhat threatening to free private enterprise.

Since some Labour party leaders were also quietly moving toward endorsement of regulation of the market rather than establishment of a command economy, to some degree the two parties were moving toward a central position.

Independent research organizations also exhibited increased interest in planning. One of these was the National Institute of Economic and Social Research. The appearance of an article on Soviet planning in its *Economic Review* in November, 1959, indicates a belief that the topic was pertinent to the British scene. A year later, in November, 1960, there appeared a publication which attracted much wider attention. This was the volume *Growth in the British Economy,* published by another influential independent organization, Political and Economic Planning. It had been in preparation for three years by a small research group including a student of government, two academic economists, and a few individuals drawn from industry.

After dismissing as beyond its scope possible attitudes of managers and workers inimical to technical change, the report discussed some of the other factors thought by its authors to have been responsible for Britain's relatively slow rate of growth. Among these it stressed: (1) the impact of tax policies on incentives and funds for investment; (2) the absorption of productive resources by government defense and social services expenditure; (3) the illogical pricing policies of the nationalized industries; (4) the impact on longer term prospects of policies adopted to deal with immediate problems of inflation and the balance of payments; and (5) the perverse influence of inflation itself on the level and distribution of investment.

In the penultimate chapter, after brief recognition in general terms that in France much more than so-called "indicative planning," a mere indication of goals, is used to accomplish the fullfillment of the economic plans, the authors nevertheless concluded that "the mere publication of an estimate of the possible achievement of the economy for a few years ahead, if such an estimate has been carefully drawn up with the cooperation of the people who will be responsible for its realization, may in itself be a potent force making for success." To avoid distorted emphasis, the authors added: "Just as important as the publication of programmes for investment and expansion as a guide to investment decisions and as an impulse towards a faster growth of output, is the testing of many other aspects of policy against the needs of economic expansion." Finally, the report argued the need for cooperation between the government and "both sides of industry" (i.e., labor and management) to work out a wages policy which would insure that the annual percentage rise in wages did not exceed the percentage rise in productivity.

Perhaps the omissions from the report are as indicative of the trend of thinking in Britain as are its suggestions. It contains no mention of such factors inimical to rapid growth as the multiplicity of craft unions each protecting its own bailiwick; the absence in Britain in 1960 of legal minimum standards concerning provisions for compensation to workers made jobless by technical change, and of public responsibility for their retraining; or the presence in some industries of conditions sheltering inefficient firms. Nor did it discuss such a striking aspect of French planning as the discriminatory use of fiscal, credit, and other measures to favor technically progressive firms at the expense of less efficient ones. Perhaps the authors presented only suggestions for change which they thought consistent with basic British institutions. In any event, they ignored factors such as these.

Since the policy tendency of these two organizations has been fairly consistently in favor of increased government intervention in the economy, their interest in planning is not surprising. Significant of the national consensus, however, is the fact that business organizations also showed a new interest in planning. The Institute of Directors organized a visit to the Soviet Union by a group of its members in August, 1960, to study Soviet planning. The Institute is a voluntary association of company directors, with a membership of more than 41,000, which has been described as "the bosses' trade union." Among its purposes are to "support the cause of free enterprise" and to create a climate of opinion more favorable to directors. When the P.E.P. report appeared the *Banker's Magazine* (November, 1960) urged that the report "should be regarded as essential reading for all those who form, carry out, or comment upon economic policy in this country." In the same month the F.B.I. (Federation of British Industries) held a conference on "The Next Five Years" which attracted much attention.

Early in 1960 a group of industrialists and economists had formed a dining club to discuss various problems of national and business policy, including economic growth.[1] This dining club discussed and favored "indicative planning." One of the six discussion groups into which the F.B.I. conference was divided, chaired by Sir Hugh Beaver, then president of the F.B.I., was to deal with "Economic Growth in Britain." F.B.I. members who were also members of the dining club gravitated to this group, and its report reflected the conclusions worked out in the dining club discussions. While its report was not necessarily the policy of the F.B.I. as a whole, in the ensuing national discussion it came to be regarded as such, and without protest by the Federation.

The group's report, after noting Britain's relatively poor rate of growth during the postwar period, urged that government and industry should make "a more conscious attempt to assess plans and demands in particular industries for five or even ten years ahead," as had already been done for the steel industry by the Iron and Steel Board. On the basis of these assessments, government and industry might see "whether it would be possible to agree on an assessment of expectations and intentions which should be before the country for the next five years." The report sharply criticized government Stop-Go policies because of their harmful effects on confidence and on industrial investment planning. A series of letters appearing in the *Times* from January 5 to January 9, 1961, presenting some of the themes of this conference and of the P.E.P. report, attracted considerable attention.

In the following month a debate on the economic situation occurred in Parliament (reported in *Hansard,* February 6 and 7, 1961). The differences between the parties concerning the nature of desirable economic planning foreshadow vaguely the differences between the planning institutions evolved from 1962 to 1964 under the Conservative government and those being shaped in 1965 on the foundations of the previous ones by the government formed by Mr. Harold Wilson in October, 1964. Mr. Douglas Jay for the Opposition attributed the existing crisis to "the complete decontrol of the economy, and the complete abandonment of all planning." Noting the discrepancy between the steel and motor car industries' estimates of future demand, he said: "Surely it would be better if all these great industries at least worked to consistent targets, agreed in consultation with the Government, even if those targets were not always precisely achieved."

Mr. Anthony Crosland, continuing the Opposition attack, suggested that "the first thing is that the Government should define the target for growth over the next five or ten years; secondly, the Government, in the public sector of industry, should plan and coordinate investment in a way that fits in with the target; thirdly, the implications of this target, and of investment in the public sector, should be discussed with private industry so that it can plan its own investment programmes rationally."

Mr. Harold Wilson, speaking as "shadow chancellor," noted that if productivity increased by only 3 per cent per annum, national production in 1970 would have to be 42 per cent above the 1960 level to maintain full employment, and suggested that on the basis of this target the government should "draw up a series of investment programmes in the key industries, both public and private . . . designed to ensure the necessary rate of expansion, and the selective expansion of the industries which can make the best contribution to essential investment, and to exports." In an article in the *New Statesman* in the following month (March 24, 1961) Mr. Wilson suggested three ways in which the government should influence investment in the private sector: first, by taxation policy; second, by guaranteed orders; third, "where a firm refused to meet the demands placed upon it by the national programme, state-owned competitive factories would be set up."

Two features of Mr. Wilson's proposals in the parliamentary speech and this article were sharply rejected by Conservatives. "We cannot achieve such a programme without physical controls," he said. And, "It will mean taking a great deal more of the essential commanding heights of the economy into public ownership." He also emphasized that one purpose of the plan should be "to ensure . . . real social justice." Although since the "Butler revolution" in Conservative policy the party had officially emphasized social justice as one of the basic goals of public policy, Conservatives tended to stress it less than did Labour party leaders.

In response to the Labour attack, Conservative members of Parliament stressed one aspect of economic problems and policy which Labour speakers had largely ignored, the dangers of an adverse balance of payments and the need to protect sterling. Clearly, they saw in the attitudes of Labour leaders some threat to sound monetary policies. However, the Conservatives endorsed some versions of planning. The Chancellor of the Exchequer asserted that a substantial amount of planning was already being done through policy concerning public investment and monetary policy. He acknowledged the need for better planning in the public sector. Mr. Maudling, president of the Board of Trade, noted that if a single coordinated forecast was wrong it might produce a mammoth error, but agreed that it was "worth considering whether the Government and industry together can find ways of improving our forecasting of demand, because on the forecasting of demand all rational planning must depend."

In two conferences held in April, the national discussion was continued. A number of economists meeting in a Business Economist Group's Conference expressed pessimism concerning the prospects for economic growth. And the National Institute of Economic and Social Research held a three-day conference at which three French officials described the functioning of the joint government-industry groups which prepare French plans (but apparently not that part of the iceberg beneath the surface of the water, the instruments by which the French plans are executed). On the last day of the conference, Sir Robert Shone, who had been a member of the advisory group assisting in preparation of the P.E.P. report, of the dining club, and of the F.B.I. discussion group, summed up: "Much thinking in terms of three or four years ahead is necessarily done by industry. The French experience in bringing these plans as well as those of the public sector together, and determining national

policy on the basis of a four-year investment plan, throws up possibilities for this country." Sir Robert was an executive member of
the governmental Iron and Steel Board, which after the denationali-
zation of steel by the Conservative government exercised some supervision over the industry. Formerly he had been general director
of the wartime Iron and Steel Control Agncy and after the war
director of the British Iron and Steel Federation. His views are of
interest not only because of his position but because he was subsequently selected as director-general of the staff of the National
Economic Development Council.

This type of planning was endorsed again in a semiannual economic survey in the F.B.I. *Review* for June 1961.[2] The article approved a type of planning which was not Soviet "dirigisme" or
"Whitehall knows best" but a "collective pooling of ideas by government and industry." Planning, it was suggested, would provide
industrialists with a better information service and insure less interference in the economy by the government; both of these factors
would create greater certainty about the future, and provide an
environment in which it was possible for industry to plan ahead.
The only reservation expressed was that planning should not necessitate an increase in government control.

INCOMES POLICY

While this discussion of planning was going on, discussion was
also increasing concerning the problem of continuing price rises and
whether an income policy was needed to check them.

The concept of an incomes policy was not new. The first pay
pause proposed by a postwar government was not that which the
Conservative government was to announce in 1961. Under Sir
Stafford Cripps the Treasury had issued a *Statement on Incomes,
Costs and Prices* in February, 1948, in which it was stated that
"There is no justification for any general increase of individual
money incomes." Sir Stafford, however, did not interfere with arbitration in the public sector and stated in his 1950 budget speech
that the government had not interfered with free negotiations but
had merely put forward its views.

As concern over the rise in prices, especially in the price of
export goods, rose throughout the 1950's, many conventional eco-

nomic theorists rejected the doctrine that the push of rising costs could be the cause. They argued that the basic cause must be excessive spending caused or permitted by unsound fiscal policies or lax credit conditions.

In 1957 the government had appointed a Council on Prices, Productivity, and Incomes. The function given it was singularly academic in nature; its influence was to be purely educational. It was to report periodically on the economic situation, with particular reference to the topics mentioned in its title. Its reports were addressed to no specific ministry, nor even to the government in general. They were to be conceived of as addressed to everyone concerned with the economic situation: ministers, departments, trade unions, employers, and the public at large.

Sir Dennis Robertson, influential and able economist and the only economist among the three members, was not known for his advocacy of governmental intervention in the economy. In its first report, issued a few months after its creation, the Council viewed inflation as essentially a product of excessive demand to be met by curbing aggregate demand. Its 1958 report was less definite, and in its third report in July, 1959, the Council recognized explicitly the "cost push" factor in inflation and suggested that some means must be found of intervening at the points at which wage decisions were made in such a way as to insure that "incomes did not in total rise more than output even when the economy was fully extended."

The report considered a suggestion made by Lord Chandos for a five-year agreement between the two sides of industry to increase basic wages annually by "say 2½ per cent" in anticipation of productivity increases. Although this suggestion obviously implied limiting wage increases to the agreed figure, it was looked upon with favor by a number of trade union leaders, for it also promised regular increases in wages. Members of the T.U.C. Economic Committee cited the report as an indication that the employers were ahead of the unions in trying to get to grips with the wages problem. In the 1959 T.U.C. *Report* the unions undertook that if the government would "genuinely and consistently" endeavor to maintain full employment, they would accept responsibility for trying "to prevent inflation by wage settlements." Perhaps this rather surprising general statement was based on an implicit assumption that by economic planning the rate of increase in productivity would be stepped up sufficiently so that the unions might obtain annual wage increases of the magnitudes they had been obtaining, but without inflation. Or perhaps the statement was made with some reservations about the difficulties that would arise when the discussion became specific. Certainly, when the T.U.C. leaders later considered policies of wage control they came bluntly up against the fact that they not only could not control or commit their affiliated unions but also within limits must reflect the views of those unions. As the discussion proceeded, the attitude of the trade union leaders became markedly different from that stated in the 1959 T.U.C. *Report.*

In 1960, when Amory's credit squeeze did not check the rise in prices even though temporarily it checked the rise in production, other analyses of the conditions necessary for price stability began to circulate.[3] Various of these analyses, while differing in detail and on whether an "income policy" would be necessary or effective for price stability, agreed that for price stability output must be held sufficiently below capacity so that unemployment would be higher than it had been on the average in the 1950's. Paish, for example, though 2¼ per cent necessary. One aspect of the doctrine was that in this looser situation economic growth would proceed at a maximum rate and the balance of payments would, or might, be in equilibrium.

However, the government was unable to accept a policy of permitting higher unemployment. Its perception of the political limits on the amount of unemployment that could be tolerated, combined with a sense of the political inexpediency and in the minds of some individuals also the wrongness of forcing unemployment by fiscal and monetary policy for this purpose, led to a search for some alternative method of limiting wage increases and obtaining price stability.

In the spring of 1961 a report prepared by six eminent economists for the Organization of European Economic Co-operation [4] supported the cost-push theory of inflation. It too was of influence in convincing government officials and specifically Selwyn Lloyd, who was then chancellor, of the necessity to tackle the problem of wages.

In 1961 C.O.P.P.A.I. also returned to the topic. While its fourth and final report, embodying the results of its studies during this and the preceding year, was not issued until a few days after the Chancellor announced new proposals in July, he was of course aware of the studies as they proceeded, and they too undoubtedly influenced his thinking. During 1960 C.O.P.A.A.I. had made a study of attempts to control wages in other advanced industrial democracies. In January, 1961, the Council had issued an open invitation to organizations in Britain to express their views. The final report presented the information on attempts to control wages elsewhere and quoted extensively from materials assembled by the Joint Economic Committee of the United States Congress and from the Organization of European Economic Co-operation report. After agreeing that holding down demand was an inadequate means of controlling cost-inflation, the report concluded that "the alternative can only be to find ways of adjusting the rise of money incomes at the points where the decisions are taken. We believe that this is necessary for the success of any policy for full employment and economic growth without inflation. Policy must also work directly for higher productivity, both as a reinforcement of other measures and as the main end in itself."

SHORT-RUN REGULATION

One final strand of concern by the Chancellor was with the method of improving the short-run regulation of the economy. A number of possible methods had been discussed within the Treasury during the last six months of 1960. None of them would reconcile the goals of protecting the balance of payments and maintaining high-level employment, but it was hoped to devise an instrument that would at least be more flexible than previous ones in moderately repressing or stimulating the economy and that would also bite in more quickly than credit controls.

One proposal, originated in the Customs and Excise Department rather than within the Treasury, was that the chancellor should obtain authority to raise or lower all consumer taxes (drink and tobacco duties and the purchase tax) between budgets by up to 10 per cent. Another was to vary the rate of National Insurance contributions. In his April 1961 budget speech Selwyn Lloyd announced the first and a modified version of the second by which only employer's contributions might be increased by a surcharge of up to 4 shillings per week. The outcry against this second device was immediate and vigorous (it would indeed be slow-acting, perverse in its effects on export prices, and slightly discriminatory against "labor intensive" industries) and it has not been used. However, the measure for variation in consumer taxes, known as the Regulator, was generally approved, and thereafter was available.

The 1961 Proposals

While these various streams of analysis and of concern were rising in the country, in the spring of 1961, another balance-of-payments crisis compelled action, and in July the Chancellor presented to Parliament a comprehensive basket of short-run and longer-run measures to meet both the immediate crisis and the causes of the recurring crises. For the short run he presented a supplementary budget which incorporated the usual short-run deflationary fiscal and credit measures and added the full 10 per cent increase in consumer taxes permitted under the Regulator.

The longer-run measures were three. One was provision for a review of the public services, to be "carried out in a way that both slows down the rate of increase in the aggregate of expenditure, and also changes the priorities to strengthen our resources and competitive power and national efficiency."

A second was a "pay pause." The Chancellor announced that periodic wage increases in the public sector would be halted or severely checked and recommended that wage increases in the private sector should be braked similarly. "Unless we have a pause in additions to personal incomes and in public and private expenditure on less essential things," the Chancellor said, " we cannot have soundly based long-term growth." He was worrying specifically about exports. The wage rises that had already occurred in 1960 and early 1961 had been followed by price rises which increased Britain's difficulty in competing in export markets, and the Chancellor undoubtedly feared a continuation of the trend.

And the third was the proposal for a "national economic developments council." After referring to existing bodies which studied developments in the economy, the Chancellor said: "I intend to discuss urgently with both sides of industry procedures for pulling together these various processes of consultation and forecasting with a view to better co-ordination of ideas and plans. . . . I envisage a joint examination of the economic prospects of the country stretching over five years or more into the future. . . . Above all, the Council would try to establish what are the essential conditions for realizing potential growth." While in this part of his speech he made no reference to an incomes policy, it is reasonable to assume that the attempt to arrive at one was one of the tasks he fervently hoped the Council would undertake.

These three themes—improvement in the machinery for planning and controlling public expenditure, the establishment of a planning body, and the pay pause, or, more broadly, the development of an incomes policy—provide appropriate headings under which to consider the evolution of economic planning during the years 1961 to 1964.

III

Reorganization of the Control of Government Expenditures

In spite of the dominating role of government expenditures among total expenditures in the economy, there had not yet been evolved effective machinery or indeed appropriate concepts for the integrated evaluation of public policies. Policies within the fields of different ministries were often rather detached and separate matters, each decided without any systematic examination of its relationship to the policies of other ministries. P. D. Henderson puts it that there was "a disposition to regard issues of policy as being normally if not necessarily decided by a somewhat stylized process of quasi-diplomatic bargaining between ministries."[1]

Although the Treasury had the function of supervising expenditure policies, its actions were governed by the venerable attitude that its prime duty was to curb the spending of other departments. It was organized to do even this only in the small—to accomplish what has been referred to as "saving candle-ends." Up until World War II, the rule of at least several generations[2] was still in force, that even though a new spending program or project had been included in the budget and approved by Parliament, every item of subsequent expenditure within it, even for a gross of pencils, had to be approved by the Treasury before being made. Only levels of expenditure which had become routine escaped an item-by-item Treasury scrutiny. Besides retarding the execution of new programs, the rule reduced the efficiency of administration by leaving the final itemized control over nonroutine expenditures to someone not substantively responsible for the results. The rule was relaxed

26

during the war, but partially reimposed after the war's end, so that it impeded adminstration even in 1960. Moreover, the practice (if not the concept) seems to have persisted that proposed new programs need sharp scrutiny but programs that have justified themselves and become routine do not. It is fairly clear that even up to 1960 the Treasury conducted no adequate comparative reevaluation of government programs in the large or in the small from time to time. The Treasury had no unit with the function of making comparative analyses nor any staff available for them. Neither was the function effectively lodged elsewhere in the government. The prime minister lacked a staff which might perform it. At times of conspicuous change there were *ad hoc* reevaluations. But for these too the machinery was weak. Even the "candle-ends" rule had not covered the nationalized industries. As they developed, no general principle for evaluating their pricing or spending or investment policies existed, and none was developed. Some made profits, others incurred losses, and the differences were fortuitous, not the result of any social or even merely narrowly financial principle.

No doubt these anomalics created some uneasiness in the 1950's. However, the major pressure for improvement in the planning and administration of public expenditure arose simply because during the 1950's public expenditures, apart from those for defense, had been rising slightly more rapidly than national income,[3] and many Conservative party spokesmen were convinced without a substantive analysis that the trend had to be checked.

THE PLOWDEN REPORT AND ITS IMPLEMENTATION

The sharp criticism of the existing machinery presented in July, 1958, in the Sixth Report of the (Parliamentary) Select Committee on Estimates, entitled *Treasury Control of Expenditure,* was the immediate stimulus to action. Because of the confidential nature of the problems and data to be studied, the Treasury rejected the recommendation for an outside committee, but in the summer of 1959 appointed an internal committee headed by Lord Plowden, an industrialist who had served as chief planning officer in the Treasury when that office had existed under Sir Stafford Cripps. The report of the Plowden Committee was private, but its substance was published in July, 1961.[4] Its major recommendations were: that the requirement for Treasury postbudget approval of items of expenditure should be ended or the limits of exempted expenditures greatly raised; that, instead, efficiency should be attained by improving departmental administration; that regular comparative reevaluation of all of the components of public expenditure, and of their total relative to the room left for private expenditure, should be instituted; and that the Treasury should be reorganized to assume the responsibility.

In considerable part the recommendations have been put into effect. The "candle-ends" rule has been greatly relaxed. By 1964 no postbudget approval was required for items in military research and development projects up to about 100,000 pounds, for public buildings projects up to about 200,000 pounds, and for main road schemes up to a much higher level.[5]

An improvement in departmental administration, the Plowden Report suggested, would require that department heads—permanent secretaries—should value being effective adminstrators rather than ignoring administration in favor of roles as advisers to ministers. Needless to say, this is a recommendation not easily put into effect, since top civil service personnel are almost a self-perpetuating group and their values do not change on command.

Projections of Expenditures

To carry out a regular comparative evaluation of public expenditure programs, it was recommended that estimates of expenditures for a period of years ahead under existing and planned government programs should be made regularly. These should be laid alongside an estimate of aggregate national product for the same future period, and within that frame of reference an evaluation made of the components, old and new, of public expenditures relative to each other and relative to the room left for private investment and consumer expenditures. The expenditures of nationalized industries, it was noted, should be included in the evaluation.

The projection of public expenditures called for were made in 1961, 1962, 1963, and presumably also in 1964. The first two, being a new type of exercise, may have been somewhat rudimentary and casual. They were not published. However, the government decided to publish the December 1963 projections of expenditures in 1967–68. The two preceding annual exercises, plus the growing awareness on the part of department heads that they would eventually be held to account annually for a comparison between actual expenditures and earlier projections, had improved the quality of the projections. The December 1963 projections, which included investment but not operating expenditures by the nationalized industries, indicated an increase of 17½ per cent in expenditures between 1962–63 and 1967–68. No accompanying projections of national income or gross domestic product were published. While the target increase in gross domestic product of 4 per cent per year would yield a greater increase of national product than that projected for government expenditures, trends of the recent past in national product would not. The five-year projections, alongside this knowledge and the Labour party proposals for increased social welfare expenditures, were the basis of a healthy debate during the 1964 election campaign concerning the tolerable and desirable trend of total government expenditures, and the five-year projections may become an increasingly important tool of public policy. None, however, was published in 1964.

Treasury Reorganization

The preparation of these projections of course does not necessarily imply that any basic evaluation of public expenditures has been made. As noted, the Plowden Report suggested that a Treasury reorganization was necessary for the purpose. This reorganization took place in November, 1962. The Treasury was divided into two sides with some slight interweaving of functions between them: the Pay and Management side, responsible primarily for the management of the Civil Service, and the Finance and Economic side, responsible for financial and economic policy. The latter includes three functional groups: Finance, Public Sector, and National Economy. The Finance group is concerned with management of the public debt, international financial negotiations, and foreign exchange. The Public Sector group deals with the control of government expenditures, including evaluation of the components of public expenditure and of the total relative to private expenditure. The National Economy group consists of a mixed team of economists and administrators, which represents a new pattern of organization within the government. As its functions were set out in 1962, it concerned itself with all of what an economist terms "macroeconomic" policy, that is, inflation, deflation, the price level, unemployment, long-term growth, the balance of payments, etc. In short, it covered the same ground as two organizations established in 1962 outside the governmental departments, the National Economic Development Council and the National Incomes Commission. Necessarily, it evaluated their work and made recommendations concerning the government policies about which those bodies also make recommendations. This situation does not imply unnecessary duplication. There must be official responsibility for these policies and therefore analysis of them within the government. The National Economy group also prepared the framework of projections of gross domestic product, tax revenues, etc., within which, ideally, the Public Sector group makes its evaluations.

Under the governmental reorganization carried out by the Wilson government, that portion of the National Economy group concerned with long-range economic projections and policies related to them was transferred to the Department of Economic Affairs. The implications of this realignment of functions are discussed in Chapter IX.

The Nationalized Industries

Concerning the policies of the nationalized industries, a major one-time step has been taken.

In July, 1961, when the Treasury published the substance of the Plowden Report, it also published a White Paper on *The Financial and Economic Obligations of the Nationalized Industries* (Cmnd. 1337). This had been stimulated by a request from a group of ministers who had perhaps been primarily interested in economy in the narrow sense, and this motive may also have interested Mr. Selwyn Lloyd, the chancellor. However this may be, the principles enunciated were a marked advance on the previous totally amorphous situation, even though they in turn leave something to be desired.

In general, the White Paper directs each industry to act as a commercial firm and over a five-year period make a reasonable average annual rate of return on its capital. These are defined: for

electricity, 12.4 per cent and for gas, 10.2 per cent, before allowance for depreciation; for the Post Office, British European Air-
ways, and London Transport Authority, 8 per cent, 6 per cent, and
5 per cent respectively, net of depreciation. The National Coal
Board was to break even after allowance for depreciation, and
British Railways to reduce its deficit as rapidly as possible. There
are two defects in the criteria: (1) The rates of return are set
largely with an eye to providing self-financing. Thus, the Electricity
Board is set a high rate of return because it needs a considerable
amount of funds for expansion. (2) Some bodies are to earn the
stated rates of return while including in their accounts services
which are subsidized as a matter of public policy. An example is the
provision of low rate electricity in rural areas. Neither of these criteria is completely logical. It is not equitable that current users of
electricity should pay the cost of construction of added power facilities, when covering that cost requires the Electricity Board to set
rates high enough to yield an unusually high return on its capital.
Neither is it equitable that electricity users rather than the public as
a whole should pay the cost of subsidizing rural users. Nevertheless,
the policies established in the White Paper move appreciably toward
sensible management guides.

Thus, by 1962 the government had taken great strides toward
organization and procedures by which it might plan its expenditure,
tax, and other economic policies in a way to maximize the public
welfare. Of course creation of the organization appropriate to a new
function does not necessarily imply the performance of the function.
It would be surprising if the Treasury had immediately begun to
carry out fully effective evaluations of public expenditure policies,
for three reasons. The first is that the criteria for a true comparative
evaluation among governmental expenditure programs, and between them and the private expenditures which in a full-employment
economy they displace, are so vague that the judgments which must
be made are extremely uncertain. A second is that to execute the
function new attitudes would have had to be created in the Treasury,
and new attitudes are not created quickly. Finally, execution of the

new function would make the Treasury a superministry, a supervisor of the policies of all other government agencies. That it should have the function of pinching pennies was accepted, but that it should make major substantive policy decisions would be strongly resisted not only by the civil service staffs of all other ministries but by the other ministers. Even though there are strong arguments for placing the function within the Treasury, since it is intimately related to other Treasury functions, it can probably be done effectively only by an office of the prime minister himself or of a deputy prime minister who is regarded as more than first among equals. Such an office did not and does not exist in Britain, except as the Ministry of Economic Affairs is now being given the role.

Hence, although the Treasury obtained five-year projections of expenditures from the various government departments it did not in fact carry out the evaluations for which the projections were to have been one basis. So, at least, states Robert Neild, former deputy director of the National Institute of Economic and Social Research and now economic adviser to the chancellor. In an article written in 1964, before he entered the Treasury, he states that while expenditures are totaled up and perhaps scaled down, there is not yet a costing of alternatives and presentation of choices to ministers (*Listener,* August 27, 1964).

IV

The Formation of the National Economic Development Council

The concept of a national economic development council may well have come from the prime minister, Harold Macmillan, who while he had been chancellor had been an economic "expansionist" and who later as prime minister had been groping for a way of arriving at a national consensus which would be a solid base for economic policy. In any event, a policy of this importance was of course a policy arrived at after discussion among the government as a whole.

The history of establishment of the council is a history of tripartite bargaining among the government, the trade unions, and the employers' organizations. The bargaining took place against the background of intense discussion in the press.

Much of that discussion dealt with the relationship between planning and productivity. One fairly common view suggested, often without spelling out the links by which the two were thought to be joined, that the planning of attainable future levels of output and the related probable demand for various types of goods would increase the rate of advance in productivity in Britain. The logic seems seems to have been that an increased rate of investment, to be attained through planning because coordinated judgments of the anticipated level of demand would show that an increase in capacity was justified, would result in an increased rate of advance in productivity. This school made no clear distinction between investment for expansion, that is, mere construction of added productive capacity, to serve an anticipated larger market, and investment which involves advance in techniques and thus results in a faster rate of increase in output per worker or of improvement in products. The first, of course, brings no improvement in the economy's competitive position except as economies of scale are gained from enlarged plants. It seemed to be assumed that the first type of investment would automatically include the second, but this extremely shaky assumption was not explicitly stated. Rather, fairly often there was simply a failure to distinguish between the two.

A minority school argued that independent stimulus to advance in productivity is necessary to make planning work. Some proponents of this viewpoint saw the competitive stimulus which would result from joining the Common Market as precisely the necessary ingredient. An article in *The Director* (September, 1961) saw planning as unnecessary if the stimulus to competition which would be provided by Common Market membership was injected. The article suggested that the government's proposals to set up planning machinery, "though well-intentioned, will prove ill-timed," because when Britain had entered the Common Market that in itself might have "resolved" the sterling issue.

Alongside this very general discussion of the relationship of planning to advance in productivity there appeared much discussion of the appropriate nature of the planning institutions. The discussion was complex, but the numerous threads in it related to the various aspects of a single central issue. Sometimes clearly seen, sometimes lost in confusion of detail, the issue was whether the planners would be responsible to the government or to private economic groups. One view of planning visualized as the central planning organization a body dominated by government officials or by independent experts appointed by the government. This body might well be advised by a group of high level representatives of the two sides of industry. It would certainly need extensive contact with representatives of specific industries or industry groups to obtain the benefit of their experience and judgment, and their views would certainly affect analysis of what was feasible. But after listening to the advice of either these individuals or the higher-level spokesmen for special interest groups, and considering the biases involved, the central body would exercise a final independent judgment in drawing up a development plan and recommending policies to further it. The other vision was of a central body representing the various economic interest groups in the country, with government officials added primarily for liaison. It was to be hoped that, hearing the collective judgment of the men most intimately acquainted with the problems of production and producers, the government would give weight to it and act accordingly.

The Chancellor met representatives of the Trades Union Congress on August 22, and of the employer's organizations (the Federation of British Industries, the National Association of British Manufacturers, and the British Employers' Confederation) on the following day. The Trades Union Congress (T.U.C.) represents almost all British unions,[1] but it has no power to bind any of its members. Membership in the employers' organizations is open to all employers. However, these organizations have often been led by individuals whose views may be more farsighted and more "activist" than those of some rank and file members.

The Chancellor put forward the two alternative suggestions for the structure of the proposed planning body which have just been outlined. Whether the council was to be composed predominantly of independent experts serving the government or of interest group representatives, he proposed that it should be supported by a permanent staff of economic experts whose function would be to prepare reports on national requirements for discussion by the council.

He was left in no doubt of the preference of the two groups with whom he met. They desired a body representing themselves, and indeed indicated no interest in cooperating with any other. The government was prepared to concede the independence of the council from the government without argument, not merely because it was obvious from the discussions that it would not gain the cooperation of either side of industry if it did not, but also because the chancellor himself, Mr. Selwyn Lloyd, unlike senior Treasury officials, favored such a body.[2]

The T.U.C. leaders expressed other reservations about the government's plans. There were three general sources of trouble. In the first place, the trade unions suspected that the government's avowed commitment to planning was a mere political tactic, halfhearted and opportunist. They were doubtful whether planning without controls, to which the Conservative party was obviously opposed, could ever be effective. In this suspicion and this view concerning controls they reflected an attitude expressed more widely within the Labour party. "A party which does not believe in controls can't believe in planning," Mr. Wilson told the Labour Party Conference in October. (*Financial Times,* October 8, 1961.)

Second, the trade union leaders felt that they should be allowed a far greater share in the formation of economic policy than they suspected the Chancellor was prepared to allow them. And, third, they had no intention of seeming by any acquiescence in the government's planning proposals to endorse the pay pause. They demanded its end.

The Chancellor tried to reassure them concerning their role, in a letter which he sent to them and the representatives of the employers' organizations on September 23. He wrote: "I am anxious to secure that both sides of industry, on whose co-operation the fulfilment of our objectives must significantly depend, should participate fully with the Government in all stages of the process. . . . They would . . . have better opportunities to help in the moulding of the economic policies of the Government at the formative stage."

The N.I.E.S.R. conference in the spring of 1961 had given a group of key men a general acquaintance with the French planning model. Subsequently, the N.I.E.S.R. organized a visit by a number of influential officials to France in October (when the Chancellor was about to have his second meeting with each of the two interest groups) to study French methods of planning on the spot. The party included five representatives from the Treasury, two from the Board of Trade, several leading industrialists, financial journalists, and a representative from the T.U.C. Research Department. Among these individuals were Sir Edward Boyle, then economic secretary to the Treasury and later minister for education in the Conservative government, Mr. R. W. B. (later Sir Richard) Clarke, at present head of the National Economy group of the Treasury, and three future members of the N.E.D.C.: Sir Robert Shone, Professor E. H. Phelps-Brown (then a member of C.O.P.P.A.I.), and Mr. J. M. Laing.

An interesting result of this visit was the abrupt change it brought about in the *Economist's* attitude toward the relationship between the Treasury and N.E.D.C. Editors of the *Economist* (October 28, 1961) were so favorably impressed by the influence an outside body had managed to exert in France (so they interpreted the French planning procedures) that they revised their previous opinion that N.E.D.C. should be closely tied to the Treasury. They also felt that the system of detailed industrial consultation in France had some lessons for Britain, but that there was danger that it might breed restrictive practices.

Late in October the Chancellor met for a second time with the representatives of each of the two interest groups. One of the major requests of the employers at this time was for a guarantee that the supporting staff of the proposed council would be entirely independent of the government (and thus entirely controlled by the council). They wanted to avoid the possibility that the government might exercise any control over the council by controlling its staff. The Chancellor agreed readily to the complete dependence of the staff on the council. Indeed, all of his meetings with the representatives of the employers' organizations went smoothly, because there were few divergencies between his views and theirs.

The trade union leaders insisted, like the employers, that the staff of the council should be responsible solely to the council. They also suggested that council members should not merely be selected from the leaders of economic interest groups, but also should be representatives of these groups. From the start, the unions had indicated that they expected N.E.D.C. to be an arena for bargaining among interest groups, and that union leaders who joined would regard themselves as representatives of the unions. They made it clear that they were opposed to the representation of outside advisers such as economists, precisely because they were "divorced from the centre of power."

On learning of this attitude of the trade union leaders, the *Economist* (in the issue of October 28, already cited above) expressed its misgivings concerning the prospects for the success of the council. In supporting the creation of a body independent of the government, the *Economist* was advocating a council of technical experts, not representatives of economic interests. "If this conglomerated body of competing vested interests does try to be the main plan-making authority, striking a compromise on every issue, the planning simply will not work." The overriding impression they had received concerning French planning, the editors added, was that its success could be attributed to the fact that the *Conseil Supérieur*, a small body weighted heavily with government ministers but including also representatives of the nation's economic interest groups, had held virtually no meetings during the first fifteen years of its existence. If a council consisting of representatives of economic interest groups were to become initiator of planning (its supposed function), the results would be disastrous. The function of planning, the *Economist* asserted, should be to diminish the power of organized groups and increase the influence of economic technocrats over government policy. The editors added a specific comment about the T.U.C.: it would be difficult to have much confidence in the T.U.C. as an active partner in the planning machinery so long as it continued "to turn its blind eye so deliberately on all the most difficult planning subjects within its own immediate sphere of interest." The *Financial Times* three days earlier had more briefly voiced similar misgivings. The two papers reflected the uneasiness of various other observers.[3]

Nevertheless, in the final arrangements, announced in January, 1962, the Chancellor found it necessary to concede most, if not quite all, of what the trade union leaders wished. Apart from the director general of the supporting staff (which was to be known as the National Economic Development Office) only two members of the twenty-member council were to be independent experts. The members drawn from the employers' organizations were to be selected as individuals, in no formal sense responsible to their organizations for the positions they took on the council. However, the trade union members, rather than being named by the Chancellor, were to be selected by the General Council of the T.U.C. When the General Council voted in January to join the N.E.D.C., it did so with the reservation that the trade union representatives were to be free to raise any subject for discussion within N.E.D.C. and to report back to the General Council. They were thus clearly to act as representatives of the trade unions rather than as independent individuals.

Both the trade union leaders and the employers apparently were uneasy lest the government seek in some way to impose its contractionary economic viewpoint on the National Economic Development Council or the Office, for example by appointing as director general of the Office someone who would be subservient to its views. To relieve this fear, on December 18, the Chancellor announced the appointment of Sir Robert Shone. His appointment was greeted as a victory for "the expansionists" as well as for those in favor of an independent body.

It was suggested above that the trade union leaders were sensitive to the charge that they might implicitly be endorsing the government's wage policy. This was a final major issue which they raised with the Chancellor. Since he had linked together in a "package deal" his restrictionist short-term measures, the pay pause, and his proposals for a new form of planning machinery, giving support to the planning proposals might seem to be assenting to the pay pause as well.

Their indignation at the pay pause was enhanced by the fact that the Chancellor had imposed it only three months after granting a cut in surtax. In his 1961 budget, in April, he had announced the raising of the level of income at which surtax would start from 2,000 pounds to 5,000 pounds. The change "was privately welcomed by almost everyone who knew anything about taxation, irrespective of political party" [4] and it was accompanied by an increase in the profits tax from 12½ to 15 per cent, which might be regarded as a counterweight, but this attracted far less attention. It was generally agreed that the change in surtax without some conspicuous compensating measure such as institution of a capital gains tax had placed the government in a difficult tactical position in its negotiations with the union leaders, since it placed them in turn in a difficult position with respect to their unions.

At the initiation of negotiations the trade union leaders had therefore been extremely eager to include wages in the discussions about N.E.D.C., and to obtain a commitment for the end of the pay pause. They raised the issue sharply at their first meeting with the Chancellor in August. He responded by reaffirming the necessity for the pay pause. The *Observer* (August 27, 1961) reported that the T.U.C. leaders came away from this meeting "looking grim, but feeling elated by a sense of unity which they had not felt for years." The *Observer* also suggested that it would be necessary for the Chancellor to make some political gesture, such as the announcement of his intention to introduce a capital gains tax, if the support of the union was to be won. Some businessmen admitted privately that they would be prepared to "readjust" their attitudes to such things as a profits tax, if it would help to put N.E.D.C. on its feet.

The tactic adopted by the Chancellor was to try to separate the wage control issue from the N.E.D.C. discussions, without yielding concerning it. Admittedly, this would leave the N.E.D.C. an incomplete planning body, for planning without either wage controls or measures which would bring about price stability in the absence of wage controls would obviously be incomplete. However, he apparently thought that the choice facing him was to detach the wage control issue from N.E.D.C. or obtain no N.E.D.C. In retrospect, this seems correct. It seems doubtful that any counterbalancing measure by the Conservative government would have induced the trade unions to endorse the pay pause or the later "guiding light."

The *Financial Times* (October 17, 1961) stated: "It seems inevitable that wage planning will become part of the responsibility of the proposed N.E.D.C. . . . It is recognised in Government circles that it is unrealistic to try to plan for growth without making any provision for planning incomes. But for tactical reasons it is apparently felt that for the time being the two policies must be developed separately."

This evasion of the issue was not fully successful, for the T.U.C. leaders still insisted on termination of the pay pause.

By the time of the second meeting of the T.U.C. leaders with the Chancellor, on October 25, the situation had deteriorated as a result of the Government's refusal late in September to implement a pay award to 2,300 Admiralty employees made by an industrial court. However, early in November the T.U.C. was thought likely to vote to join N.E.D.C. and when the Electricity Council (the governing body of the nationalized industry) on November 16 granted a pay increase which violated the pay pause, on November 20 the T.U.C. Economic Committee drafted a letter of acceptance.

The Electricity Council action had not, however, reflected Government policy. With the Prime Minister in Scotland and the Chancellor in Paris, the chief negotiator for the Electricity Council had told the Minister of Power by telephone of his desire to make a wage settlement violating the pay pause. The Minister of Power, without informing either of his absent colleagues, had simply told the negotiator that he, the negotiator, must take the responsibility. The wage agreement violating the pay pause was then announced. However, on November 21, a day after the T.U.C. letter of acceptance had been drafted, in a speech in Parliament the Prime Minister sharply rebuked the Electricity Council and announced that the wage pause would continue. On the following day, the T.U.C. General Council rejected the draft letter, specifically because of the government's reaffirmation of the pay pause. The trade union leaders asked how, in the face of such a policy, the N.E.D.C. could be expected to operate democratically. Mr. George Woodcock, general secretary to the T.U.C., was quoted the following morning as asking: "If the Government does not listen to us about a short-term measure like the pay pause, then how do we know that the Government will listen to us on a long-term matter like planning?" (*Financial Times,* November 23, 1961.)

In loftier tones, the *Times* of the same morning emphasized that the setting up of an economic planning body provided an opportunity for the Chancellor to act "as the Champion of the Nation as a whole," and criticized him for making a distinction in his economic policies between those who were "well to do" and those who were "less favourably placed."

An impasse had then been reached in the negotiations: neither side was prepared to make concessions before they were sure that the other side would reciprocate. The trade unions wanted a firm date for the end of the pay pause; the government wanted a guarantee of union cooperation on N.E.D.C. On December 18, when announcing the appointment of Sir Robert Shone as director general of N.E.D.C., the Chancellor reemphasized that the consideration of plans for expansion rather than a wages policy was the prime function of N.E.D.C. and agreed to consult the unions on wages. However, these gestures were not sufficient. On December 21 Mr. Woodcock was reported to have said that the T.U.C. could not "go on havering" (a Scottish word which means to be indecisive) and should vote against joining N.E.D.C. because the Chancellor was "not handling the problem in the right way."

The impasse was broken in January by an exchange which reflected private negotiations. On January 6, 1962, the Chancellor agreed to send the T.U.C. details of the "intermediate phase" of his incomes policy. (This presumably referred to the "guiding light" announced the following month.) On January 10 he wrote to the T.U.C. urging that it join N.E.D.C. On January 17 the T.U.C. Economic Committee voted in favor of joining, and one week later, the T.U.C. General Council ratified this recommendation. At this date it was generally reported that the government intended to terminate the pay pause on March 31, and no doubt a firm assurance had been given to the T.U.C. An official statement was issued on January 30.

The Labour party had apparently pressed the T.U.C to join, one of the reasons being concern about the "image" the party would present at the next election.

On February 8 the Chancellor announced that in addition to the president of the Board of Trade, the Minister of Labour, himself, and Sir Robert Shone, the Director General, the Council would have sixteen members, including two prominent in the academic world, two representatives of nationalized and six of private industry, and six trade unionists whose names would be announced later in the month. One of the representatives selected by the T.U.C. was Mr. Frank Cousins, general secretary of the Transport and General Workers' Union who had vigorously opposed the entire proposal. Mr. Cousins was to become Minister of Technology in the Labour government in October, 1964.

V

The Functioning of the National Economic Development Council

The Council held its first meeting on March 7, 1962. In the early probing of attitudes among the members, the representatives of employers' organizations were critical of their own organization and attitudes, and stated their awareness of the need for adaptation. The president of the F.B.I. spoke of the need for both sides of industry to reexamine their positions: the T.U.C. should look at its structure, and the employers should try to make their own positive contribution to the problem of wage inflation by concentrating on methods of alleviating the shortage of labor, effecting an improvement in training programs, relieving housing shortages, and establishing more adequate redundancy provisions.

The trade unions, after expressing their views on controversial issues, announced their readiness to adapt themselves to the requirements of planned economic change. They felt that N.E.D.C. should accept a better distribution of existing wealth as one of its objectives. They acknowledged that if its program was to be implemented a "response to the challenge would be required from trade unions and employers as well as the Government." Genuine economic planning would require changes in the functions of the trade unions. "If everything is in, we will not be afraid of discussing at N.E.D.C. what part wages can play in a plan for genuine progress." (*Labour*, October, 1962.)

The two sides thus manifested good will. However, when specific policies were discussed in later months, difficulties appeared.

43

A FEASIBLE RATE OF GROWTH AND THE OBSTACLES TO IT

At the first meeting of the Council, the Chancellor had outlined his conception of its functions as follows: (1) to examine the economic performance of the nation with particular concern for plans for the future in both the private and the public sectors of industry; (2) to consider together what are the obstacles to quicker growth, what can be done to improve efficiency, and whether the best use is being made of our resources; and (3) to seek agreement upon ways of improving economic performance, competitive power, and efficiency—in other words, to increase the rate of sound growth.

"I do not want this to be a body," he stated, "which just listens to Government decisions, and is merely asked for comment. I want it to have an important impact on Government policy during the formative stage, and upon the economic life of the nation. I believe that it can."

At the second meeting, on May 19, the program of work to be put before the Office was discussed. It was decided that the director general should prepare a report to be published at the end of the year on the following subjects: (1) general economic implications of the growth rate in the next few years—for example, the implications for exports, balance of payments, savings, investment, and manpower; (2) impact of the rate on a selected cross-section of industry; and (3) study of general obstacles to growth and of economic policies and industrial arrangements and attitudes in so far as they may affect growth.[1]

The period adopted for the study was 1961 to 1966, because projections could then be based on figures available for 1961. A target growth rate of 4 per cent per annum was tentatively adopted as a basis for the calculations. While it was based on work in the Treasury, N.I.E.S.R., and under Professor Richard Stone at Cambridge, it assumed an increase in the previous rate of growth. This increased rate was hardly more than an optimistic rough and ready rule of thumb, adopted because no less a rate seemed sufficient to solve the country's problems and no higher rate seemed at all plausible. It is true that trade associations and other industry groups were asked whether they could attain a level of output consistent with the increase assumed for the economy as a whole, but their affirmative replies seem to have been expressions of faith or of good intentions, rather than conclusions based on technical analysis. Some members of the Council (presumably the employer members) were apparently reluctant to adopt the 4 per cent rate without further study, and it received no official sanction until developing unemployment underlined the need for growth.

Unemployment had been aggravated if not caused by the deflationary measures adopted by the government in July, though a cyclical retardation of economic growth may have been impending when the 1961 measures were introduced. From a low of 1.4 per cent in the second and third quarters of 1961, the national average level of unemployment rose to 2.5 per cent in the fourth quarter of 1962, and within that national average were concealed percentages of 3.6 in Wales, 4.3 in Scotland, and 7.0 in Northern Ireland. In November, leaders of the T.U.C. met with Mr. Maudling to impress on him their view of the seriousness of the situation. By January, 1963, the effects of the bad winter were further aggravating the situation. This deepening unemployment had its impact on N.E.D.C., and on January 24 N.E.D.C. announced that the 4 per cent target suggested by the Office had been accepted as a firm objective. For the government, Mr. Maudling accepted the objective.

The *Financial Times* (January 25) commented: "The events of the past year have made it seem likely that Britain, like the U.S., can maintain full employment only if the economy grows at a faster pace than in the recent past."

A very sharp rise in production was needed during 1963 to make up for ground lost in 1961 and 1962 and to keep the level of unemployment down to 2 per cent. An even sharper rise in exports—one sufficient, the Office suggested, to give an average annual increase of 5.7 per cent during the five-year period—would be needed to offset the rising demand for imports as demand and production rose. It seemed that the point had been reached when the government might decide that it was better to risk a sterling crisis than the continuation of unemployment at a relatively high level. At the beginning of February Mr. Maudling announced his determination not to introduce any economic or employment measures which might have to be reversed later. That is, he declared the end of Stop-Go, a significant reversal in Conservative party policy.

So much for the target rate of growth. A comprehensive statement of the obstacles to foster growth and the policies needed to overcome them was more difficult to arrive at.

At its third meeting, in June, 1962, the Council had urged the staff to make a preliminary assessment of the "conditions favourable to faster growth" as soon as possible. Verbally, it will be noted, the emphasis had shifted from "obstacles to growth" to a positive approach. The nine subjects to be studied were: the balance of payments, savings and investment, demand, regional problems, manpower, management, technological change, taxation, and public expenditure. "According to reports after the . . . meeting, the Council found itself in complete accord in identifying the 'growth obstacles' which have to be examined, and there was no real disagreement over points of detail. . . . The air of amity which appears to have characterized the first three meetings may reflect the tactful manner in which Sir Robert Shone and his Office have presented their suggestions, and the fact that the Council has not yet got beyond the programming stage." So wrote the *Financial Times* (June 7, 1962).

In the period between the third and fourth meetings Mr. Selwyn Lloyd was succeeded as chancellor by Mr. Maudling. Though in 1960 Mr. Maudling had been one of the leading critics of the N.E.D.C. concept, he had by now fully accepted it. Much of the fourth meeting was spent discussing the significance for the balance of payments of a faster rate of growth. The Office was instructed to study the matters discussed, and to put forward suggestions uninhibited by traditional views. At the opening of the meeting Sir Robert Shone announced that his preliminary report concerning conditions favorable to faster growth should be ready by October. This, he stated, should "signal the end of the period in which the Council has merely been preparing its broad programme of work, and may lead to more frequent and decisive meetings during the winter."

At October and November meetings of the Council the draft report was considered, but no conclusions were reached about the policy statements contained in it.

The Council met on three days in February, 1963, and announced that the report on the general economic implications of the economic growth visualized for the priod 1961 to 1966 would be published in March. There was no agreement upon when to issue the third section, on obstacles to growth. There was opposition to the draft of this section from trade unionists, particularly Mr. Cousins, who felt that inadequate time had been devoted to the study of wider issues (e.g., prices and incomes policy) which might require consultation with rank and file trade unionists. The union leaders, moreover, were critical of the export target, even though it had been scaled down to 5 per cent per year. They may have feared that measures to increase exports might include some of which they would disapprove, for example, wage controls.

The press was severely critical of the fact that there was still no agreement to publish the third part. The *Guardian* managed to obtain a copy of the draft prepared by the Office and published it on February 20. After further editing by N.E.D.C., it was finally published as a separate report entitled *Conditions Favourable to Faster Growth* on April 18. Comparing it with the draft, the *Financial Times,* April 18, 1963, expressed disappointment at the fact that some parts of the draft report had been altered and one section dropped altogether. The subject of an incomes policy, the *Financial Times* noted, was only discussed in very general terms and no mention was made of the part which the National Incomes Commission established in 1962 would have to play in incomes restraint. The proposals for tax reform were put forward cautiously and the section on the balance of payments bore signs of being "a compromise dictated by the Treasury." There was no discussion of restrictive practices. The most fruitful parts of the report were the sections on regional unemployment and planning, concerning which the interests of the Council members were most similar. "All this compromise," the *Financial Times* suggested, "shows that N.E.D.C. is now at the cross-roads. The initial work of sounding industry and inviting a report has now been completed, and the great question is: what does N.E.D.C. do now?"

The survey of export trends, which had been discussed at the April meetings of the Council, was published in June. This report, too, was severely criticized by the *Financial Times,* this time for its ambiguity. It was not clear whether N.E.D.C. felt that to improve export performance would require restraining costs at home (i.e., by an incomes policy, etc.) or whether more drastic measures were necessary, such as special export incentives or even devaluation.

"There are obvious difficulties in the way of discussing these issues publicly," the *Financial Times,* May 6, 1963, said: "While Neddy leaves its conclusions deliberately ambiguous, however, the value of its reports will remain smaller than it might have been."

At its October meeting the Council considered a preliminary report prepared by the Office on Britain's progress toward a 4 per cent growth rate. This report, *The Growth of the Economy,* was published in March, 1964. It noted that the greatest deviation of actual events from the projections had been a serious shortfall in exports. Actually, output also failed to reach the 4 per cent trend line. Even the surge in the fourth quarter of 1963 brought output only up to a level 8 per cent above the average for 1961, a rise of 3.5 per cent per year. (The further rise in 1964 was at about the same annual rate.)

"Little Neddies": The Second Stage of Planning

At the first meeting of the Council, Sir Robert Shone had stated that in recruiting the staff of the Office he was planning two divisions: one to deal with broad economic questions and the other to concentrate on the problems of particular industries and sectors of the economy. The former would deal with economic growth and stability in the nation as a whole, while the latter would organize and maintain relations with the Economic Development Committees or "little Neddies" which were visualized for individual industries.

It had early been realized that the prospects and problems of individual industries must be studied and that committees for liaison with individual industries must be established. Soon after the formation of N.E.D.C. seventeen industries from the public and private sectors had been chosen for study. They were selected primarily because they were industries for which information was already available, but also because they covered the whole range of the economy. Those in the public sector were coal, electricity supply, gas, and the post office; those in the private sector were agriculture, chemicals, chocolate and sugar confectionery, building, civil engineering and building materials, heavy electrical machinery, electronics, iron and steel, machine tools, motor vehicles, paper and board, petroleum, wool textiles.

In the autumn of 1961 discussions had begun within the building industry, one of the industries whose ailing condition was the most obvious, about setting up a special council of the organizations allied to building to form a liaison committee between the industry and N.E.D.C. when N.E.D.C. should be established. Shortly after N.E.D.C.'s second meeting, it was announced that ten organizations connected with the industry had agreed to serve on an "economic planning advisory council" for the construction industries. A similar organization was formed in the heavy electrical equipment industry in October, 1962, when it was announced that the four largest firms were forming a joint office to further the development of the industry and to act as a link between it and N.E.D.C. However, these councils were not "little Neddies" but rather were organizations purely within industry.

The formation of Economic Development Committees or "little Neddies" had been discussed at some length at the May 1963 meeting of N.E.D.C. These were to be committees subordinate to N.E.D.C., each relating to an individual industry or industry group. Thereafter the Office moved the plans forward in discussions with the two sides of some of the industries concerned. At the October Council meeting, it was decided that each Economic Development Committee should have about fifteen members, representing management, unions, and appropriate government departments. Their terms of reference were agreed upon in December. They were to have three main tasks. First, each must improve the quality of information available concerning its own industry as a basis for better forecasts. Second, each should examine N.E.D.C.'s plans and progress along them in relation to its industry and diagnose where the plan had gone wrong. Third, each should discuss topics of particular interest to its industry, which might in exceptional cases be discussed in N.E.D.C. as well. It is noticeable that insofar as each was to probe into obstacles to accelerated technical progress—one of the two fundamental economic problems, the other being inflation—this was subsumed implicitly under other heads. It was not mentioned as a major task.

These terms of reference were formulated only after eighteen months had elapsed since the first meeting of N.E.D.C. Six months later, two years after N.E.D.C.'s first meeting, the first five "little Neddies" were announced: they were for chemicals, electronics, machine tools, paper and board, and chocolate and sugar confectionery. The last seems to have been thrown in simply because it was easy to form. Four others were announced before the formation of the Labour government in October brought some change in N.E.D.C.'s operations; they were for the distributive trades, electrical engineering, mechanical engineering, and wool textiles.

Since the "little Neddies" might well have been a crucial instrument both for obtaining an estimate, industry by industry, of the possible acceleration of advance in productivity above past trends and for probing and attacking obstacles to an increase in the rate of advance, it is reasonable to ask why their formation was so delayed. One avowed reason was the difficulty of finding members of sufficient stature who were not already on N.E.D.C. or other existing industry agencies. Since there were only six trade union members and six managers of private industry on N.E.D.C., and since it is not immediately apparent why duplication of membership with other industry bodies would be a disadvantage rather than a decided avantage, this reasoning is not entirely persuasive.

Another reason, which is a partial explanation of the absence of "little Neddies" for some important industries, is the existence of a vigorous "sponsor department" within the government. In such industries, both that department and the industry felt some fear that a "little Neddie" would displace existing arrangements for consultation.[2]

The sponsor department system developed during World War II (it may have existed in some degree before the war) and has survived since. The sponsor department administers laws and regulations relating especially to the industry and, on the other hand, if the industry has an inquiry or a problem relating to any government department or agency, it comes to its sponsor department and that department handles the matter.

For most industries, the sponsor department is the Board of Trade. Its role is typically passive; it performs only the functions just described. However, where government regulation is extensive or the government is the industry's main customer, the role of the sponsor department may go much further. Thus, the Ministry of Agriculture is a very active sponsor department. The Ministry of Aviation has forced mergers of aircraft firms. Toward the end of the Conservative government's period in power, the Ministry of Public Works and Building and the Ministry of Housing and Local

Government took promising initial steps to induce local housing authorities to coordinate their contracts for housing construction so as to offer a long run of construction for contract, thus permitting production and construction economies. The two ministries also took steps to induce construction firms to respond.[3]

It is indicative of the concern about interference with established relationships that when the Economic Planning Advisory Council for the construction industry was formed by N.E.D.C., it was agreed that this Council would not "stand in any way between the organizations representing various sections of the industries and those Government departments where machinery for consultation already exists." It is significant that none of the nine "little Neddies" formed by the end of 1964 covered a nationalized industry (e.g., coal, gas, electricity, railroads) or one with an active sponsor department.

It should be noted that the nine that were formed did cover important industries. If to those industries are added agriculture, the aviation and construction industries, and electricity, gas and coal, where a direct link with the government was already present, then machinery existed eventually by which either N.E.D.C. or the government, so far as either was so minded, could probe into problems of productivity in all but a few of the country's important industries.

However, this explanation is incomplete. It does not account for the extreme delay in the formation of "little Neddies." Not only was N.E.D.C. preoccupied with other matters. Most members of N.E.D.C. did not regard the formation of Economic Development Committees as of the first importance. Obviously, trade union leaders and industrialists who had themselves found it difficult to probe into such matters as labor restrictionism, sluggishness in management, or, perhaps, management cartel arrangements, might not see great advantage in creating new bodies to do so. If some members of N.E.D.C. possessed an imaginative view of the functions the "little Neddies" might perform, such a view was not effective in the Council as a whole.

Apart from discussions of incomes policy (mentioned in the section following), these were the main activities of N.E.D.C. up to the defeat of the Conservative government in the October 1964 elections. It had, however, been more than merely a discussion group. The management and trade union representatives on N.E.D.C. had reached agreement on government action concerning the training of workers, on the setting by government of compulsory minimum standards for compensation to workers who became superfluous, on important changes in the National Insurance scheme, on more active measures for regional development to replace the limited and not very imaginative development certificate scheme, on measures to assist the movement of workers, on the need for expanded management training, and on the need to couple discussions of prices with an incomes policy, among others. In each case, a change of some importance in the attitude previously taken by the trade unions or management or both was involved. These agreements had facilitated and in some cases had largely motivated actions by the government. (Most of these matters are discussed in later sections of this book).

The meeting place provided for top men from the two sides of industry and the link between the government and the "men of action" had considerable value, and in the future may have great importance.

VI

The National Incomes Commission

When it had become clear that the trade unions would not accept an incomes policy as part of a National Economic Development Council package, the action of the Conservative government was forthright. In a White Paper, *Incomes Policy: The Next Step,* issued in February, 1962, the government announced a continuing incomes policy. After the termination of the pay pause at the end of March, wages were not to rise by more than 2½ per cent per year. This policy became known as the "guiding light."

Trade union leaders of course immediately denounced the policy, and it had little effect in private industry. The government applied it with some qualification in the public sector, but as pay rises in that sector lagged farther and farther behind those in private industry, and consequently labor shortages and the threat of strikes increased, the policy came to be breached increasingly even in this sector in 1963 and 1964.

FORMATION OF N.I.C.

Meanwhile, since the trade union members of N.E.D.C. had refused to have anything to do with the Chancellor's incomes policy, the government moved to establish alternative machinery.

In July, 1962, five months after the announcement of the "guiding light" and four months after N.E.D.C. had come into existence, the government took the first step. Following a meeting with union leaders, the Chancellor announced a proposal for a national incomes commission. The final form and terms of reference

53

of the commission were not announced until November, after meetings with the unions.

Representatives of the employers' organizations welcomed the proposal because they felt it would help the country to achieve expansion without inflation. Trade unions vigorously opposed it, on two grounds. First, they stated that the government had shown no signs of giving up its restrictionist economic policy; and second, they argued that the T.U.C. could not be associated with any body which might have the right to interfere in the policies of the affiliated unions. As the negotiations continued, the trade union leaders asserted that the government was concerned with its own political survival, not with expansion, and that N.I.C. represented wage restraint dressed up in a new form. Mr. Woodcock said that if wage increases were to be denied on the grounds of Britain's international position, then "the Government is the only body which can take the responsibility for this decision, and suffer its political consequences." (*Labour,* August, 1962.)

His response and that of other trade union leaders was not entirely negative, however. In the article just quoted Mr. Woodcock went on to say that he set himself "the ambition to achieve . . . a more sensible, more just, and more ordered system of regulating wages and incomes," and that this could only be done through tripartite discussion on the whole range of government policy. In response to the government's challenge to find an alternative to N.I.C. the Trades Union Congress in September directed its General Council to make a study of what the trade unions' attitude should be toward planning and, in particular, the planning of incomes. In addition, the General Council was directed to study the need to adapt the organization of the T.U.C. and the individual unions to suit modern industrial conditions. Mr. Woodcock exerted a moderating influence in the discussion. He promised that if N.E.D.C. could produce a comprehensive scheme of economic planning for growth then the unions would see what part wages could play in this plan. He warned the union leaders that their members would have to display a "responsible attitude" to wage claims in a planned economy, and emphasized that it was essential for the union movement to remain inside N.E.D.C. But it was clear that the unions would have nothing to do with the National Incomes Commission.

The Opposition leader, Hugh Gaitskell, claimed that the government had made the same mistakes over setting up N.I.C. as it had over the pay pause. It had failed to set the incomes policy in the context of an overall policy for economic expansion and had not made sure that it was comprehensive and fair.

It was obvious that a commission composed of representatives of interested groups could not be formed. Whether solely for this reason or because the government preferred a commission of experts, such a commission was created.

In November it was announced that Mr. Geoffrey Lawrence, Q.C., would be the chairman of the proposed commission, which would include three other members: a solicitor, an accountant, and a professor of industrial relations. According to the terms of reference, the commission might consider: (1) any current claim on pay or conditions referred to it by the parties concerned; and (2) claims referred to it by the government, where the cost would be met in whole or in part by the Exchequer. The government might also refer any private settlement, except an arbitration award, to the commission for *retrospective* examination. The commission itself was to take evidence from the parties concerned and any other relevant evidence. It must publish its findings and recommendations, giving reasons for them, and it might advise the government to take fiscal or other measures to restrain profits.

In considering a claim the commission must "have regard both to the circumstances of the case concerned, and to the national interest." Specifically, as criteria the commission was to consider "the desirability of keeping the rate of increase of the aggregate of money incomes within the long-term rate of increase of national production," the desirability of paying a fair reward, the manpower needs of the industry, its policies and practices on prices, profit margins, dividends and efficiency, and "the repercussions which a particular settlement in the case concerned might have in other employments." There were to be no sanctions except that of public opinion.

DECISIONS BY N.I.C.

On December 11 the Chancellor referred to the commission for retrospective examination a recent agreement whereby Scottish builders and plumbers would get reduction in the working week from 42 to 40 hours with no loss of earnings.

The N.I.C. announced that it was ready to receive written statements from anyone interested in the settlement and later would probably take oral evidence in public. It was understood that the employers' organizations were ready to cooperate, especially those south of the border, who felt that they would be in a stronger position to resist their own employees' demands for a shorter working week, However, the national secretary of the Building Section of the Transport and General Workers' Union said that the unions would not be deterred from their "normal activities" even if N.I.C. did condemn the settlement, and on January 23, 1963, the T.U.C. advised the building unions to boycott N.I.C.'s hearings. The Scottish building unions were reportedly disappointed at this advice, since they felt they had a good opportunity to embarrass the government by arguing for a shorter working week in the light of the rising trend of unemployment in Scotland. Although they did not give their evidence to N.I.C., they later published it. The commission took evidence from a government team including representatives of the Treasury, the Ministry of Labour, and the Ministry of Public Building and Works, and from the Scottish Plumbing Employers, the National Federation of Building Trades Employers, the Civil Engineering Constructors, and the Scottish Building Employers' Federation.

The commission's report on the settlement was issued on April 22, 1963, slightly more than four months after the case had been referred. The commission announced that the Scottish building settlement could only result in an excessive and inflationary increase in wages and therefore judged it to be contrary to the public interest. They recommended that the settlement be abrogated by agreement or, failing that, that the Scottish building workers should be given no wage increase until the rise in national productivity justified a two-hour reduction in the working week. They recognized that there were special circumstances leading to the plumbers' claim, and suggested that they should have a straight increase in wages. (There were other minor and more positive recommendations concerning future procedures in the industry.)

The commission, in making these recommendations, had noted that the customary current method of negotiating wage increases was defective, because the national interest was not represented. An editorial in the London *Times* on the morning following publication of the report drew attention to the way in which N.I.C. had put its finger on "several delicate spots" N.E.D.C. had hardly touched upon. It was not sufficient, the *Times* argued, for the negotiating parties to have the joint interests of their own industry at heart "in the context of today's conditions in which sustained growth and full employment without inflation are the desirable objectives." Though keeping incomes in line with productivity might necessitate restraint for a short period, in the long run it would facilitate growth, and thus incomes could rise faster.

The unions' reaction was that N.I.C.'s report was an "impertinent interference" in their negotiations. Opposition came from both manual and white-collared unions. The report was seen as a "threat to negotiating machinery" and "foreign to any reasonable conception of democracy." Neither did the employers' organizations fully endorse the N.I.C. recommendations. They said that the commission's advice was valuable, but that it remained the responsibility of the employers and the unions to settle the claim.

However much managers may have agreed with the specific recommendations, their attitude toward them as an operating principle was demonstrated by the fact that while discussion of the Scottish settlement was still in progress, there was a rush of 40-hour week agreements.

At the same time, N.I.C. began to receive criticism from independent bodies. N.I.E.S.R. submitted a memorandum to it, suggesting that a "guiding light" should be set not by prudent accounting but by a realistic strategy. It should be "an essay in psychology" designed to secure acceptance of an incomes policy. A report of the Royal Economic Society, published in March, stated that Britain's economic effort was being hampered by lack of research into the effects of economic policy decisions. An incomes policy had been embarked on with inadequate knowledge, and export expansion plans were based upon untested assumptions.

In his speech on April 5 on Mr. Maudling's 1963 budget, Mr. Macmillan made it plain that it has been designed in an attempt to secure union cooperation on an incomes policy. He outlined the tax concessions made to the lower-income groups and publicly adopted N.E.D.C.'s target for wage increases (3–3½ per cent), higher than the Treasury's "guiding light" (2½ per cent). The *Financial Times* (April 6, 1963) expressed its belief that, with the exception of a small minority, most of the unions' leaders recognized the responsibility which had been put upon them. The trade union leaders, however, failed to respond.

In December, 1962, in recognition of the commission's need to carry water on both shoulders, the F.B.I. had sent a letter to the Chancellor. Its theme was that an effective incomes policy must cover all forms of income, hence it was just that profits and dividends should be included; but, it added, these forms of income are essentially different from wages and should be controlled by general economic and fiscal policy.

At the beginning of March the government referred to N.I.C. wage agreements reached in the exhibition industry, in domestic engineering and the industries installing heating and ventilating equipment, and in the electrical contracting industry. The commission published its report on these cases in July. The report discussed the question of profits, but without accepting the F.B.I. view. One chapter was devoted to a discussion of the general issues involved in an incomes policy. It stated that a survey of pricing, profit margins, and dividends in the separate branches of the construction industry was urgently needed. Profits could be as inflationary as wages. The cooperation of firms would be necessary for such a survey to be made, and without it N.I.C.'s reports on wages would be disregarded, and the commission would be accused of being one-sided. Shortly afterwards the Chancellor issued a statement to the effect that he had already consulted the F.B.I. about means of obtaining a more detailed breakdown of the figures provided by the trade associations.

Building contractors of course rejected the idea of investigating profits. Any hopes that the T.U.C., on the other hand, might be converted to N.I.C. by its second report were dashed. "It is not what they say, but the body that says it to which we object. . . . N.I.C. is an unrepresentative body with no standing. It has neither the competence nor the authority to deal with either wages or profits."

Two subsequent reports, in March and June, 1964, the first on the remuneration of university teachers and the second an interim report on agreements in the engineering and shipbuilding industries, added little to the development of an incomes policy. The report on university salaries recommended considerable increases, partly because under the pay pause increases had been deferred and presumably partly also because the teachers best known in their professions were likely to receive financially tempting offers of positions from American universities.

The final report of N.I.C. was issued in February, 1965, four months after the Wilson government had taken office. It dealt with wage increases in engineering and shipbuilding which had been referred to the commission fourteen months earlier. Along with the discussion of other aspects of the problem presented, the commission pointed out that if an incomes policy was to be effectual it must take account not only of formal wages increases but also of "wage drift," that is, the raising of average earnings by reclassifying jobs, and in various other ways arranging to give workers more income without formal change in pay scales.

N.I.C.'s series of decisions had presented academically sound and logical discussions of the nature of an incomes policy which would best serve the public interest. They had, however, been of no effect in checking inflationary wage increases. Indeed, in anticipation that the steps being taken by the new government might lead to more effective curbs on wages, many new wage agreements granting increases had been negotiated somewhat hurriedly late in 1964 and at the beginning of 1965.

N.E.D.C. DISCUSSES INCOMES POLICY

While this work of N.I.C. was going forward, N.E.D.C. was also evidencing its concern with incomes policy. In May, 1963, it had been reported that the Office was preparing a report on the topic. In July the Council asked the Office to prepare a report on "particular issues involved, and the actual development of prices and incomes in relation to the growth programme." The impression given was that the members of the Council were slowly coming closer together in recognizing the need for some kind of agreement, but there were still difficulties over certain issues of principle.

The trade unions mentioned the lack of organization among the employers. An announcement made in July met this criticism. It was announced that the Federation of British Industries, the National Association of British Manufacturers, and the British Employers' Confederation would be replaced by a completely new body, comparable in scope to the T.U.C. The statement said that the past decade had seen much development in the determination of government to control the national economy. It added: "In the context of a rational incomes policy this involves discussion—and may lead to action—simultaneously affecting wages and other forms of income, or prices," and that an organization which could speak for all of industry was needed. The formulation of a constitution and operating structure took some time, but the new body, the Confederation of British Industries, opened its offices on August 2, 1965.

At its December 1963 meeting the Council discussed schemes designed to instill a greater sense of collective responsibility in those who fix prices and incomes. T.U.C. leaders left the day's discussion impressed by the readiness of some employers to agree that an incomes policy must consider profits as well as wages.

Proposals for taxing profits to insure that they did not move up too quickly had been put forward, but both sides accepted the view that such a policy might reduce the incentive among companies to increase their earnings.

In January, 1964, the employers' representatives put forward preliminary proposals for an attack on the problems of inflation through voluntary action by industry through a Prices Commission and a profits tax whose rates would increase as profits rose. Unfortunately, after further examination of these proposals, a special committee of the F.B.I. concluded that both schemes were administratively impracticable. This meant that although the employers expressed a sense of responsibility about prices and profits, they had no concrete proposals to offer to the T.U.C. in exchange for wage restraint. By March, 1964, the discussions in N.E.D.C. on the short-term problems of maintaining economic growth without inflation had been brought back to their starting point. Though there was continued discussion at later meetings, no specific proposals emerged. Here the matter stood when the Labour government took office in October.

The discussion at the December 1963 meeting of N.E.D.C. prompted the first expression of strong right-wing antiplanning attitudes. The most vigorous statement of the viewpoint was by Mr.

Enoch Powell, an ex-member of the Conservative cabinet. The gist of his argument was that "wages, profits, prices are determined, always have been determined, and always will be determined until we go communist, by the market—by supply and demand working through the market. While we tie ourselves in knots trying to invent non-market criteria for our commissions to use, the market is there, noiselessly, efficiently, irresistibly doing the job for us all the time." (*New Society,* February 6, 1964.) Relatively few businessmen, however, identified themselves publicly with this point of view.

VII

The Labour Government's Quiet
Revolution in Planning

At this stage in the development of N.E.D.C. and N.I.C., when the one had demonstrated a somewhat limited vision of its role and the other spoke clearly but impotently, the Labour party gained power, even though by the barest of majorities The new government immediately made some changes in the government's organization to deal with economic affairs. One of Mr. Wilson's first acts was to create two new ministries: a Ministry of Technology with the function of accelerating the pace of technical advance in certain important industries, and a Ministry of Economic Affairs with a far broader responsibility for so changing the nation's economic performance that it would achieve all of its major economic goals— an accelerated rate of advance in productivity and income, price stability, and improvement in the balance of payments. To head the Ministry of Economic Affairs, he named his former rival for the Labour party leadership, Mr. George Brown. At the same time he named Mr. Brown Deputy Prime Minister and First Secretary of State. To head the Ministry of Technology he named Mr. Frank Cousins, General Secretary of the country's largest union, the Transport and General Workers' Union, and one of the leaders of the Labour party's left wing. Mr. Cousins did not resign his union position; rather, he requested and was granted a leave of absence.

During the months which followed, the activities of one governmental department after another were expanded somewhat or redirected in part, or both. These changes will be discussed as the programs involved are discussed in this and the following chapter. In passing, one other aspect of the reorganization of the administrative structure may be mentioned here. This is the recruitment to governmental service of a fairly large number of economists from the universities. To an American, both the desire of the British government to expand its staffs of economic analysts and the response of academic economists to the call are reminiscent of the call for economists and the trek of American economists to Washington in response during the first year of Franklin Roosevelt's New Deal. The British influx, however, has been much smaller relative to the size of the governmental establishment and it has attracted much less public attention. The lesser attention may be due simply to the fact that the use of economic analysts in governmental planning is no longer novel.

The recruitment has occurred at two levels, within the regular civil service and in super- or extra-civil service positions. The appointment of a number of economists by the Ministry of Overseas Development is a rather special case of expansion of economic analysis at the civil service level; these economists are not working on planning in general. However, not only the Department of Economic Affairs but also those of Transport, Aviation, and Defence have brought in added economists.

More striking has been the appointment of Mr. Robert Neild as Economic Adviser to the Chancellor, Mr. Nicholas Kaldor as part-time adviser on tax measures in the Department of Inland Revenue, and Mr. Thomas Balogh as Economic Adviser to the Prime Minister. Mr. F. T. Blackaby, in an essay discussing the administrative changes, notes that these three men plus Sir Donald MacDougall, Director General of the Department of Economic Affairs, consult together unofficially, and suggests that they "provide a rather irregular element of consultation between the Ministries and the Prime Minister." [1] This spontaneous development may be considered to compensate in part for the absence of a coordinating staff in the prime minister's office.

The National Plan: Numbers for 1970

By the spring of 1965, six months after Harold Wilson had been called by the Queen to form a government, the outlines of a new attack on the problems of economic stability and growth were visible. The *National Plan,*[2] a White Paper published five months later, in September, presents a comprehensive summary of the new program as far as it had then been formulated, plus suggestions of measures to be worked out. Most of the policies announced had been evolved and presented to the public during the preceding eleven months. The September document is the vehicle for surveying the measures rather than for initially presenting them. But that document will provide a convenient framework for discussion of the planning that had gone on.

Promptly after his appointment as Secretary of State for Economic Affairs, Mr. Brown took command of the planning function formerly performed by the National Economic Development Council. N.E.D.C. (on which the Secretary of State for Economic Affairs replaced the Chancellor) remained closely associated with the work, but it became clear immediately that the plan for 1970 would be an official government plan, which that prepared by N.E.D.C. had not been and could not be. Moreover, Mr. Brown took over not only a central function of N.E.D.C. but also much of its staff. To form an Economic Planning division within the Department of Economic Affairs he took over from the National Economic Development Office most of the staff of its Economic division, together with the director of that division, Sir Donald MacDougall, who was named Director General of the Department.

The plan was prepared not merely by that division or the Department of Economic Affairs (D.E.A.) as a whole, but by all of government, with the close cooperation of N.E.D.C. and with much additional detailed advice—but only advice—from industry and labor. D.E.A. created an interdepartmental committee, which in turn spawned many subcommittees to prepare drafts of sections. At the end of February, D.E.A. and N.E.D.C. jointly sent out to the "little Neddies" and trade associations an "industrial inquiry." The inquiry presented an assumption of a 25 per cent increase in the nation's output between 1964 and 1970, an increase which may perhaps be regarded as the highest that it seemed feasible to propose. On the basis of this assumption, the government requested a series of estimates from each industry. For each year from 1964 to 1970 an estimate was requested on the industry's production, the shares going to the home market and to abroad, imports of the same products, the industry's investment, its employment, its consumption of fuels and raw materials, and various breakdowns of these estimates. Some information was requested for 1970 only, for example the share of raw materials needed that would be imported. D.E.A., acting alone, addressed similar requests concerning each nationalized industry to its sponsor department.

Replies were requested by the end of March. This schedule obviously precluded much study by the respondents, but since most of them had replied to a somewhat parallel request submitted by N.E.D.C. in the autumn of 1964, they had already done relevant analysis. Improvement of the industry estimates of course continued after March. On receipt of the estimates, the Department tested them for consistency both by testing them against a computerized model of the economy developed by Mr. Robert Stone of Cambridge and in more pedestrian ways, revised them in consultation with each industry concerned, and filled in gaps with respect to types of production not covered by the inquiry. Meanwhile discussions of policy went forward.

An outline of the plan was submitted to N.E.D.C. early in the summer, before this process was far along. NE.D.C. members protested its sketchy nature at that stage, and N.E.D.O. subsequently submitted drafts expanding the content of some sections. Mr. Brown had initially expected to present a plan for the years 1965 to 1970 to the public by the end of July, but soon realized that this timetable was unrealistic. By the end of the summer there had been evolved a skeleton picture of what the composition of output in 1970 would be if the goal of a 25 per cent increase above 1964 was attained; of the problems that the nation and its producers would face in trying to attain that level of production and in trying to attain a surplus in the balance of payments; and the changes in governmental policies which, in the view of the planners, would contribute to attaining both goals. The *National Plan,* presented to the public on September 16, concluded that the production goal and simultaneously an annual surplus of 250 million pounds in the balance of payments by 1970 were attainable.

The projected 25 per cent increase in output during the six-year period 1964 to 1970 corresponds to an average annual rate of increase of 3.8 per cent, compounded. The task of attaining this rate is increased by the low rate of growth of the labor force. During the decade 1955 to 1964, the labor force had increased by some .6 per cent per year. However, because of the distortion of the nation's age distribution resulting from deaths and low birth rate during two world wars, by 1970 the increase in the population of working age will come almost to a halt. The average increase in the labor force during the period 1964 to 1970 will be only .25 per cent per year. This will be true, that is, unless participation in the labor force by persons of working ages is somehow stepped up. It is noted in the plan that the regions of highest unemployment are also those of lowest participation in the labor force, and it is suggested that the provision of added job opportunities in those regions may draw into jobs not only 50,000 unemployed but also 150,000 persons not now seeking work. But even on this rather optimistic assumption, the average annual rate of increase in employment in the nation as a whole would be only .4 per cent. To attain the increase in output called for in the plan, the average annual rate of increase in output per worker would have to be 3.4 per cent.

While this rate is slightly less than that hoped for in the N.E.D.C. projections for 1961 to 1966, it is far above the actual rate of 1960 to 1964, and indeed far above that of any five-year period in Britain's history.

However, the rate has been rising. The increase in productivity from 1963 to 1964 was some 3 per cent, and from 1964 to 1965 may have been 3.25 per cent. The industry projections for the period 1964 to 1970, in combination, indicate an annual increase for the economy as a whole of 3.2 per cent. Possibly, rather than being overly sanguine reactions to an assumed goal of a 25 per cent increase in aggregate output, these are reasonably realistic forecasts of continuation of a high rate of advance. If they are, the government's task is to raise the average rate of increase in productivity .2 per cent per year above the rates projected by the various industries, remembering, however, that the projected rates may reflect the anticipated effect of many governmental measures. An alternative way of attaining the production goal might be to obtain an additional increase of 200,000 in the labor force by inducing housewives to take jobs or persons at retirement age to continue to work, or, rather, by inducing employers to offer jobs to such persons. However, an increase in the labor force would not contribute to increasing exports whereas an increase in productivity, which implies a reduction in costs or an improvement in products, would do so.

Perhaps, it was suggested above, the projections of increases in productivity are realistic. But perhaps they are not. "Industrialists," the *Times* (October 4, 1965) states, "have had plenty to chuckle about in the sections of the plan relevant to their own industries." How can planning be done on the basis of such uncertain projections?

In analyzing any plan that is cast in the framework of attainment of specified quantitive goals, there is some tendency to regard the figures presented as the heart of the plan. With respect to the balance of payments goal in the Labour government's plan, that emphasis is justified. It is a matter of the gravest economic importance for Great Britain to demonstrate to the world that successive devaluations of her currency will not become necessary. The prerequisite to that demonstration, in the present context, is that *no* devaluation shall take place. For if any devaluation were found necessary, after the pledges of 1965, who would have great confidence that there would not be further devaluations later? The attainment in the intermediate future, or say by 1970, of a surplus in the balance of payments sufficient to give assurance that repayment of Britain's international debts will be completed reasonably soon is a minimum condition for the necessary international confidence. And manifest progress toward that goal during the intervening years is a further condition.

But with respect to domestic production, the emphasis on a specific goal, a 25 per cent increase in aggregate output, is spurious. For the relief of various domestic economic tensions, a 20 per cent increase in per capita output by 1970 (and per capita output is what counts) offers greater promise than a 17 per cent increase. A 24 per cent increase would still better. A 28 per cent increase would be better yet. And so on. No one point on this continuum is marked *Success* whereas lower points are marked *Failure*. Nevertheless, each successively greater increase offers enough added promise of relieving tensions so that the true goal of the government should be, not any *given* production target, but *more*. That is, whatever the rate of increase in output projected in the absence of new governmental measures, the goal of the government concerned about the economy's performance should be to act so as to increase that rate—

provided only that the governmental measures are ones that aid the economy to function optimally rather than ones that achieve a temporary result at the cost of a later reduction in efficiency.

Any given rate of increase in productivity will also serve the balance-of-payments purpose better than any lesser rate, so long as the added rise in productivity contributes more to exports than the added rise in income contributes to the demand for imports. There is reason to suppose that the effect on exports will be the greater. The example of Japan is a case in point.

As soon as one turns one's attention from the production target which provides the framework for the *National Plan,* one realizes that the avowed goal is precisely that suggested above. That is, the goal is to improve the functioning of the economy, whatever the level of functioning that might seem to be in prospect in the absence of action, and to do so even though the resistances to new governmental measures may be strong.

Two years earlier, when the N.E.D.C. projection for the period 1961 to 1966 was prepared, the members of N.E.D.C. had reached agreement on some changes in the behavior of their organizations and in governmental policies impinging on those organizations that would accelerate increase in productivity. These agreements have been discussed in Chapter V. As suggested there, the employer members of N.E.D.C. were somewhat freer agents than were the labor representatives in acknowledging the need for changes. Nevertheless, the document presented to the public by N.E.D.C. is singularly silent with respect to policies that would press hard against customary practices or tread on the vested interest of any important industrial or labor group. It is clear that some members of the N.E.D.C. realized that harder choices would be required, but the need for consensus kept any but the most general discussion of some difficult problems out of the report. The N.E.D.C. "plan," therefore, has some flavor of the belief that, given a benevolent governmental environment, acceptance by business managers of a high national production goal is sufficient to cause them to achieve the productivity increases consistent with it.

The *National Plan* is free from this misconception about the results of "indicative planning." The numbers in the plan are designed as a framework for the evaluation of many policies, for example: investment plans; training programs; production goals for coal, electricity, and agriculture; plans for the construction of transportation facilities; policies for attack on industrial monopolies, on managerial complacency, on labor restrictionism. The numbers, it is implied, may improve the planning of some managers of enterprises by persuading them that their prospective market is larger than they had realized and may keep governmental ministers and leaders of industry and labor from underestimating the tasks facing them. This, apparently, is about all that the leaders of the Labour government expect of the numbers. If some economist expressed the judgment that planning for larger scale production would in itself increase productivity, the framers of the plan would no doubt agree. But the plan gives the impression that if the economist said further, "This is all that is necessary to achieve the goal you have set yourself," the framers would have replied, "Then let us see how much higher a goal we can achieve by facing the difficult problems."

To the *Economist* (September 18, 1965), which had hoped for radically new measures in some fields of the *National Plan*, the text looked "about as radical as a wet hen." The comment may reflect the fact that the document presents only generalities and statements of purpose in some areas of action in which governmental policy had not yet been formulated. But, as will be shown below, if the statement is meant to imply that the policy statements are merely platitudinous, then it is not justified.

The *National Plan*, after two summary chapters, discusses in successive chapters projections and proposed policies relating to manpower, industrial efficiency, investment, prices and incomes, the balance of payments, and regional planning. An industry by industry discussion of prospects and policies follows. The concluding section of Part I then discusses the use of resources: consumers' expenditures, housing, and the various classes of public expenditure. Part II consists of summaries, industry by industry, of the replies to the industrial inquiry, including the views of the representatives of each industry concerning public policies.

Discussion of the policies already put into effect or announced by the Labour government and those announced in the plan for future formulation occupies much of the remainder of this essay. Policies relating to productivity and the control of inflation are discussed in this chapter, regional planning in Chapter VIII, measures designed to increase the mobility of labor and to reduce the scope and power of monopolies both in this chapter and in one section of

Chapter X, and those intended to right the balance of payments in one section of Chapter XI.

INCREASING THE PACE OF ADVANCE IN PRODUCTIVITY: VARIOUS MEASURES

Expenditure Policy

To leave room for expansion of private output, the government pledged itself to limit the increase from 1964–65 to 1969–70 in public expenditures, in constant prices, to an annual average of 4¼ per cent. In a year's time, it was added, the government would review the expenditure programs in the light of economic developments and would establish a limit to expenditures for 1970–71.

The 4¼ per cent annual increase is of course greater than that anticipated for national output as a whole. The government expects to take a gradually increasing share of the nation's output for public uses. The anticipated rate of increase results mainly from planned increases in expenditures for housing, education, and road construction. It is proposed to increase total housing construction from 383,000 units in 1964 to about 500,000 in 1970. Of the houses built in 1964, 162,000 or 42 per cent were public. It is proposed that this proportion shall be increased. If the proportion is increased to one-half, a fraction suggested informally, the increase in expenditures for housing construction would be of the order of 55 per cent. A 32 per cent increase is proposed for total expenditures for educational purposes and a 41½ per cent increase in expenditures on road construction and maintenance.

On the other hand, the increase in health and welfare expenditures is to be held to 23½ per cent, or slightly less than the percentage increase in the nation's total output. Room is to be made for increases in the housing, education, and road programs by holding defense expenditures in 1969–70 to the level, at constant prices, of the 1964–65 budget, 2 billion pounds. Defense expenditure programs planned when the Labour government took office would have occasioned a considerable increase in expenditures. Most of the increase has been lopped off by canceling a program for the development of a supersonic bomber, scheduling the purchase of American bombers instead, and by reducing the size of the armed forces Reserves (an organization roughly comparable to the American National Guard). The reduction in aircraft research and development, it is suggested, will release many engineers for research in other industries.

Labor Training and Mobility

One of the products of the industrial inquiry is a forecast that the shortages of skilled workers experienced in 1965 will increase. The government reacted by expanding the work of the Government Training Centers. These agencies for the retraining of redundant works have existed since 1921. By the end of 1965, it was announced, there will be places for 6,000 trainees in the centers and later there will be expansion to 8,000 places if there is sufficient demand for the training. The course of training is about six months; the maximum annual output is twice the number of places. The expansion is intended chiefly to relieve shortages of skilled workers in construction and in "engineering occupations" (machinery production and the like). Expansion of the supply of skilled workers in these industries is necessary if bottlenecks hampering the expansion of construction activity are to be broken.

Simultaneously, the government has acted to expand rapidly the training of workers entering industry for the first time. Until the 1960's the government had regarded worker training as a matter to be negotiated between employers and unions. Very little worker training except by apprenticeship or practice on the job had resulted. Craft unions often resisted the introduction of training schemes on the ground that only apprenticeship could give thorough training, but the underlying motive may have been their reluctance to permit an increase in the supply of workers. Following the recommendations of a 1962 White Paper on the subject, an act relating to the training of workers for industry was passed in 1964 under the Conservative government but by interparty agreement. For the first time, worker training was treated as a matter of public rather than merely union and employer interest. Under the act, the government may set up an Industrial Training Board for any industry (comprised of representatives of employers, unions, and the government, plus other expert members). This board may then administer a training program financed by a tax levied on the industry.

Few boards had been established by the time of the downfall

of the Conservative government, simply because little time had elapsed since passage of the act. The Labour government has acted with some speed. By mid-1965 boards had been set up for the engineering, construction, woolen textiles, steel, and shipbuilding industries; and before the end of the year boards had been established or were being discussed in industries employing about 60 per cent of all nongovernment employees. The program has not received warm endorsement in all industries; the enthusiasm of the government for formal worker training is greater than that of some industrial firms.

In its efforts to increase the mobility of workers, the government has disregarded traditional dogmas of labor unions and employers alike. In the past the matter of severance pay for workers who become superfluous, like that of worker training, has been regarded as one for negotiation between employers and unions. Because of union insistence that the only proper principle was *no* elimination of jobs, unions have avoided discussion of the issue of severance pay. As a result, financial compensation to workers discharged in Britain because of technical or economic change has been inferior to that of most—perhaps all—of the other countries of Western Europe. Moreover, unemployment compensation in Britain has been at a uniform rate regardless of the worker's previous income. The explanation perhaps is the reluctance of unions to admit the propriety of any unemployment, plus some sort of equalitarianism. The resulting heavy cost of unemployment to higher paid workers has been one of the factors causing them to avoid the risk of even temporary loss of work.

To increase the mobility of workers, in 1965 the Labour government introduced legislation providing for lump sum payments to workers losing their jobs because of technical or economic change. The payment will be made regardless of whether or not the worker becomes unemployed. In addition, the government has increased the benefits already payable to workers moving from one locality to another. Further, the government has announced that it will introduce legislation to relate unemployment benefits to the worker's level of earnings, and that it is exploring the problems of arranging that a worker's occupational pension rights shall transfer with him when he changes jobs.

Varied Actions to Increase Productivity

A variety of programs has been designed to increase industrial productivity and the rate of increase in that productivity. Early in August, 1965, an official committee of inquiry into labor problems on the docks, headed by Lord Devlin, filed its final report.[3] The report proposes a "decasualisation" of dock labor, simultaneously a removal of various restrictive practices, and subsequently the progressive introduction of improved goods-handling devices and procedures, and suggests steps to these ends. The first steps taken under the direction of the Minister of Labour, Mr. Ray Gunter, to implement the report, seem to indicate a firmer determination and greater skill in obtaining action than had been true in previous attempts to remedy conditions on the docks, and it is possible that significant improvement will be attained.

The Department of Agriculture will intensify some of the programs of financial aid to agricultural capital expenditures which have been associated with the 6 per cent annual increase in productivity in agriculture in recent years. The income of farmers is so wholly dependent on government subsidies that action in the industry is largely controlled by government decisions. To avoid increasing imports the government will administer selective expansion of the production of some agricultural products, for example, beef, veal, milk, and cereals. The government expects that its aid to continuing increases in productivity in other fields of agriculture will be accompanied by the continued exodus of workers to nonagricultural industries.

The weaseling about the level of coal production has been ended. The government will permit coal output to fall to 170 or 180 million tons by 1970 (the exact figure depending on exports), even though this involves the transfer of workers among mines and out of the industry. The government moved late in 1965 to appoint a permanent special investigator in the automobile industry, among whose duties will be to deal with unofficial strikes, which have been a cause of much loss of production. The unions have refused to try to settle these strikes, since they are in defiance of union authority. The new investigator, who will be chairman of a council that has been set up by the industry, will have legal power to call for evidence. Now that the government has decided to treat with unofficial strikers in the auto industry, arrangements may be made to do so in other industries. The government has established two new major schools for management education. It is investigating whether it seems possible to increase the inducement to investment by altering the present system of investment allowances. It is also considering legislation to focus brighter light on management performance by requiring fuller disclosure of company operating results.

However, the most interesting new programs designed to raise the level of productivity in industry, and its rate of increase, are those being carried out by the ministries of Technology and Economic Affairs.

The Ministry of Technology

Before the election, Mr. Wilson had repeatedly asserted the especial importance of the "science-based" industries of machine tools, electronics (including computers), and telecommunications, and had stated his intention to create a new ministry with the function of accelerating technical advance in those industries. On taking office, he promptly created the Ministry of Technology, of which, as has been noted, Mr. Frank Cousins was named minister. The appointment of the brilliant and influential physicist P.M.S. Blackett as chief science adviser in the ministry, and of the novelist, science adviser in the wartime government, and company director C.P. (now Lord) Snow as parliamentary secretary, with indication that he would be concerned with problems of management, suggests the range over which the ministry intended to spread its interests within those industries.

Before his appointment as minister, Mr. Cousins had been a member of N.E.D.C. and a director of the Department of Scientific and Industrial Research, whose agency, the National Research and Development Corporation, had had the function of sponsoring research and development. This corporation was now placed under the Ministry of Technology to be used as an agency for the enhanced stimulation of technical advance. The corporation is continuing to conduct product research, but, with increased funds, it will be the vehicle by which on a bolder scale than before the government joins selected private firms—"chosen vessels"—in financing advanced applied research. The first example of this activity was a "research and development contract" with International Computers and Tabulators, Ltd., the British computer manufacturer which is the largest in Europe, by which the government will contribute 5 million pounds toward the cost of developing a new series of "compatible" computers. A group of smaller contracts with other British computer manufacturers to expedite the development of various pieces of auxiliary computer equipment accompanied it. These were followed in June by the announcement of plans for a considerable increase in research and development contracts with machine tool producers to help in the production of prototypes of the most advanced machine tools. Simultaneously the National Engineering Laboratory began work on the problems of design and production of numerically controlled machine tools.

The Ministry of Technology, it was announced, would also encourage mergers of firms in the machine tool industry into stronger units. Also, in 1965, the talents of an established and effective research agency, the United Kingdom Atomic Energy Authority, were put to new uses when the Authority was directed to do research in other fields. The first of these was desalination.

Another tool, less precedented than research contracts, has also been put into the hands of the Ministry of Technology. This is discrimination among firms, when making government purchases, on bases other than the price quoted. The first suggestion of the use of this policy is Mr. Cousins' proposal that the government shall buy machine tools only from firms which meet "required standards in sales effort, design and research, and employment policies." (*Sunday Times,* February 14, 1965.) The Conservative government had taken action to prod construction firms to improve their methods (see above, p. 50), and had relied for its influence on the fact that it and local authorities are large purchasers of construction, but it had not dreamed of discriminating among purchasers on bases other than price. If such discrimination is to accomplish its purpose, it must of course be administered with great restraint and good judgment.

In its first eight months the Ministry of Technology gave promise of imaginative innovations in policies. However, except in the research contracts initially announced, relatively little action has taken place. Moreover, the Ministry itself may not have developed the ideas for some of the promising 1965 measures. In mid-1965 the Estimates Committee of the House of Commons criticized the administration of the Ministry as top-heavy, inept, and inefficient.[4] Similar criticisms have been made by other observers. It is possible that the Ministry is failing to contribute as much as a more effectively administered department would to stimulating technical progress.

INCREASING THE PACE OF ADVANCE IN PRODUCTIVITY: THE DEPARTMENT OF ECONOMIC AFFAIRS AND THE ECONOMIC DEVELOPMENT COMMITTEES

Although selected assignments were given to the Ministry of Technology, the major vehicle for attempts to accelerate technical progress in Britain is the Department of Economic Affairs. The responsibilities of the latter department extend to the industries with which the Ministry of Technology is concerned as well as to all others. Within the Department of Economic Affairs, the division to which this broad responsibility is assigned is the Industrial Policies division.

To head that division, Mr. Brown obtained on loan from the British Aluminum Company, Ltd., Mr. H. F. R. Catherwood, its young, highly respected, innovational managing director. As his lieutenants, termed industrial advisers, Mr. Catherwood recruited other senior industrial executives plus a leading financial correspondent, all on loan rather than required to resign their career positions to accept the governmental posts. The four first appointed were: Dr. J. A. Berriman, managing director of Shell Refining Co., Ltd.; Mr. A. C. H. Cairns, chairman of Unilever Exports, Ltd.; Mr. Michael Shanks, economic correspondent of the *Sunday Times;* and Mr. I. J. Young, partner of the firm of investment consultants, Urwick Orr and Partners, Ltd., and a specialist on corporate mergers. The caliber of these first recruitments indicates both the importance given by the government to the function and the sense which these men must have of the importance of the job to be done.

The formal function of these advisers is to serve as the department's representatives on the Economic Development Committees. As before, each E.D.C. includes representatives of management and unions in the industry, a representative of N.E.D.O., a representative of the "sponsor department" of government, and independent experts. Now, a representative of the Department of Economic Affairs has been added, and in some, or all, of the "little Neddies" increased stress has been placed on the use of expert consultants to probe the possibilities of increasing efficiency in the industry. Under each E.D.C. working parties are formed for intensive analysis of specific problems. The chairman of each E.D.C. is a person experienced in industry and knowledgeable concerning the industry involved but not drawn from that industry. Each is now appointed by the Secretary of State for Economic Affairs, that is, Mr. Brown, rather than by N.E.D.C.

A steering committee to expedite the formation of "little Neddies" was formed early in 1965: it is headed jointly by Mr. Catherwood and Mr. Tom Fraser, head of the Industry Division of N.E.D.O. (not to be confused with the Minister of Transport of the same name). In June the formation of three additional E.D.C.s, the first formed since the previous autumn, was announced. Two, with a common chairman, were for civil engineering and the building industry. The third was to deal with speeding the movement of exports. It will be discussed in Chapter XI. Two others, covering rubber and processing, were created later in the summer. They brought the total to fourteen. The *National Plan* announced that by the end of 1965 twenty were expected to be in operation, covering industries employing thirteen million workers, or about two thirds of total employment in the private sector. None are planned for the public sector.

Through their membership in the "little Neddies" plus their contact with each other in D.E.A., the industrial advisers form, in British terminology, a "ginger group" to probe obstacles to more rapid advance in productivity in each industry: lack of standardization, "featherbedding," other restrictive practices by management or trade unions, lack of longer-term planning, managerial lethargy or self-satisfaction, or any other—and to work persuasively for removal of such obstacles. In a sense, each industrial adviser is being asked to extend his concern with technical progress from a single company to an entire industry or group of industries. The "little Neddies" may provide an extremely effective vehicle through which to exert the persuasion. The industrial advisers may press more effectively than could any private individual or organization for rationalization via the merger of small firms. They (and other members of "little Neddies") have encouraged interaction among "little Neddies" to work out improvements which involve interindustry cooperation. Given the high sense of public purpose which must have motivated the industrial advisers to take these public jobs, they may work more wholeheartedly for increase in productivity, even if this involves breaking restrictive practices of management or lessening job control by unions, than could any private entrepreneur. They can also obviously perform this work much more effectively than could civil servants without industrial or managerial experience.

The work of the Economic Development Committees is in the main quiet and unheralded. These committees might of course be mere discussion groups. However, from bits of comment about their work, verbal and in the press, one gets the impression that some of them are extremely effective instruments. While the industrial advisers are an important addition to the mechanism, their work alone would be rather ineffective if there were not many capable individuals caught up by the sense of national purpose in the Committees. Possibly—just possibly—this stone which many observers have neglected is becoming the cornerstone of the edifice.

Just as there remains with N.E.D.C. itself a function of great importance, namely, discussions among labor leaders, representatives of employers, and government officials concerning problems, policies, and sources of conflict, so the Economic Development Committees will perform this function for single industries or industry groups. Clearly, the removal of some obstacles to more rapid advance in productivity will be one source of conflict. The ties resulting from the performance of this parallel function at different levels will be one major future link between N.E.D.C. and its little counterparts.

Obviously, the Department of Economic Affairs has taken over from the National Economic Development Council in large part the utilization of the Economic Development Committees, in addition to having taken over the central role in the formulation of economic plans and a large part of the N.E.D.O. staff. It would be erroneous, however, to assume that N.E.D.C. is merely a vestigial organ, surviving from an earlier day. In a society as pluralistic as the British, the government cannot make plans for change and impose them. There must be interplay among the pluralistic elements in the society. N.E.D.C. will continue to be a central organ for that interplay. Indeed, it is conceivable that N.E.D.C. will be the more effective for having had taken from it a corporatist function which it could never truly have performed.

INCOMES POLICY

While the machinery for economic planning and the acceleration of advance in productivity was being established, the Secretary of State for Economic Affairs was also pressing forward the formulation of new machinery for the administration of an incomes policy. He proceeded with all "deliberate speed." By May, 1965 he had completed erection of an agency which had at least a reasonable prospect of cooperation by both employers and the Trades Union Council, a prospect which the National Incomes Commission had lacked from the day of its formation.

After discussions with representatives of the employers' organizations and the trade unions during the weeks after the formation of a new government, Mr. Brown had obtained the assent of both to a joint Statement of Intent on Productivity, Prices, and Incomes. It was signed precisely two months after the new government took office, on December 16. By it, employers and the trade unions agreed to cooperate with machinery to be established by the government for the following purposes: (1) to keep under review the general movement of prices and of money incomes of all kinds; (2) to examine particular cases in order to advise whether or not the behavior of prices or of wages, salaries, or other money incomes is in the national interest as defined by the government after consultation with management and unions.

In a White Paper issued on February 11,[5] stated to have been prepared by the government in cooperation with representatives of the T.U.C. and the employers' organizations and to have been discussed by N.E.D.C., the government indicated the nature of new institutions to be created. The government announced that it would invite N.E.D.C. to carry out the review of general prices and incomes movements (statistical data and analyses to be provided by government departments). To investigate particular cases it would establish a National Board for Prices and Incomes. This would have two divisions, for the review of prices and incomes respectively.

The Board would include a "trade unionist" and a "businessman," but since it was also to include "an independent chairman" and "a number of independent members" who will have expertise in "law, accountancy, economics, industrial relations and other relevant fields," it was clear that independent members would form a majority and that the major change from the composition of N.I.C. was the addition of one trade unionist and one businessman. The Prices Review division would be authorized to investigate any price or group of prices, including unchanged prices, in which *prima facie* some reduction may be warranted. The Incomes Review division would have a similarly broad scope. Only the government would be able to submit cases to either division. It was suggested that the Incomes Review division, with the cooperation which it was hoped that the T.U.C. and the prospective Confederation of British Industry would be able to obtain from their members, should be able to render reports within two or three months of the referral of a case.

Finally, in the White Paper the government announced its hope that persuasion and the pressure of public opinion would be sufficient to obtain acceptance of the findings of the two divisions. Nevertheless, in expressing its hope that other measures would not be necessary it reserved the right to use them. "The Government would resort to other methods," the last sentence of the White Paper states, "only if they were convinced that the voluntary method had failed." In this suggestion of last resort use of compulsion, the tone of the announcement was perhaps a tougher one than a Conservative government would have felt able to take.

In March Mr. Brown announced the appointment of Mr. Aubrey Jones, a Conservative member of Parliament, to head the National Board for Prices and Incomes. The name of Mr. Jones, a maverick within his party well to the left of many members of the party on many social questions, was reportedly a personal suggestion of Mr. Brown. The public reaction to the appointment indicated that Mr. Jones had the full confidence of trade union leaders as well as that of employers. In April Mr. Brown expressed his agreement with the view of trade union leaders that incomes control should begin with prices, not wages.

There the matter rested until the annual meeting of the Trades Union Congress at the end of April. On April 31 by a vote of more than three to one (6,649,000 to 1,811,000) the Congress endorsed the steps taken and policies announced by Mr. Brown, the one large union casting the great majority of the negative votes being Mr. Cousins' union, the traditionally aggressive Transport and General Workers Union. On the same day, Mr. Brown announced in Parliament the appointment as deputy chairman of the Board of Mr. Duncan Dewdney, managing director of the Esso Petroleum Company. This was the company at whose Fawley refinery a sufficient degree of mutual confidence was established so that in a pace-making agreement two years earlier unions had given up traditional practices which had sharply restricted productivity in return for higher pay and shorter hours. Earlier, the appointment as the other deputy chairman of Mr. Hilary Marquand, for a number of years an official of the International Labour Organization and affiliated organizations, had been announced.

Wisely, Mr. Brown asked the Board to begin its operations by examining a group of cases relating to prices: announced increases in the prices of standard bread and the flour used to make it, and in soap and detergents, and the recommendation of the Road Haulage Association to its members that they should negotiate new contracts increasing their rates. He referred these cases to the Board on May 5. The Board, promising speedy action, obtained from the firms and the Road Haulage Association agreements to defer the price rises temporarily. On June 28 the Board issued its first decision and, with the aid of Mr. Brown, won its first victory, in the case of road haulage rates.

In April, following a wage increase granted to truck drivers and a rise in the cost of gasoline because of the increase in the gasoline tax, the Road Haulage Association had recommended to its members that they negotiate new contracts with their customers providing for increases of 5 per cent in trucking rates. In assessing this action, the Board noted the recent history of costs and prices in the industry. Over a two-year period identifiable changes had increased truckers' costs by 9 per cent. Part of this increase may have been counteracted by increases in productivity such as that due to the increase in the maximum speed rate for trucks from 30 to 40 miles per hour. During the same period the Association had recommended

rate increases totaling 13 per cent. The Board suggested that ship-
pers should refuse to agree to increases of 5 per cent in rates. It also
denounced the practice of recommending uniform nationwide rate
increases. Lastly, it recommended discussions by trucking companies with their unions to revise drivers' schedules and in other
ways as well increase productivity further.

The Association announced on the same day that it saw nothing
in the report which should cause it to change its advice to members.
However, after a long meeting with Mr. Brown on the following
day the officials of the Association reversed themselves and agreed
to recommend to their members "that the principle of a general rate
recommendation should be abandoned." It was believed that many
large industrial companies thus encouraged would refuse to negotiate new rates (London *Times* and Manchester *Guardian,* June 30).

The precedent of this first victory and the powerful support
given the Board by the Secretary of State for Economic Affairs were
important. However, the victory was a modest one since it related
to price increases for which the justification was weak.

On May 18 Mr. Brown had referred to the Board a wage increase just announced in the printing and nonurban newspaper industries. The Board's second report, issued on August 18, dealt with
this case. On their face, the report said, the wage increases seemed
to violate the prices and incomes policy. However, the Board reserved final judgment until mid-1966, for in the interim there
were to be successive negotiations on various components of wage
increases covered by the contract, and in mid-1966 a Joint Manpower Committee of the printing industry was scheduled to report
on progress in increasing productivity in the industry. The Board's
report tied permissible wage increases to these possible increases in
productivity.

The report cited craft demarcation agreements and restrictive
work practices prevalent in the industry, bluntly criticized the unions
for negotiating them, and equally bluntly criticized employers for
assenting to them. It stated that buyers and specifically the government as a buyer should refuse assent to increases in paper or printing prices since by the employers' estimates increases of 10 to 25
per cent in productivity could be attained even with existing equipment. The report, moreover, condemned the escalator clauses in
the May agreement.

On September 1 the Board issued a report on bread and flour prices. They should not be increased for at least six months, the report suggested, during which period the industries should formulate proposals for the more effective use of labor. On the basis of those proposals the industry should discuss with the government the justifiability of price increases. On September 6, after talks with Mr. Brown, representatives of the bakery and flour milling industries agreed to defer price rises for three months. Mr. Brown agreed to reexamine the situation at that time.

On October 11 the Board issued a report concerning soap and detergent prices. The report found that costs had risen as much as prices between May 1964 and May 1965 including the proposed price increases. Nevertheless, since the two giant companies dominating the market, Lever Brothers and Procter and Gamble, determined prices by an inflexible procedure not closely associated with cost changes, the report argued that no price increases during the period up to the end of 1966 can be justified. The two companies promptly announced their acceptance of the recommendation.

During its first three months, the Board thus gained significant successes. Moreover, it had established a precedent of examining, in its investigations, all aspects of price and wage determination, labor restrictionism, and management efficiency. With the muscle of the government behind it, the Board's decisions were having much more impact than those of the National Incomes Commission had had.

Nevertheless, events of the prices and wages front were disturbing. When the prospective formation of the National Incomes Commission was announced, there had followed a rush to conclude agreements granting sizable increases before N.I.C. began to function. A similar event occurred during the first six months of the Labour government's tenure in office. Prices rose rapidly also, after and before wage increases. Avowedly for reasons of equity, there were rather large wage increases in several nationalized industries as well as in private industry.

There were causes of the cluster of wage increases other than the prospect of wage restraint. Large increases usually occur after a boom has stretched the economy tight. (Because of the time spent in negotiations, they often occur after a downturn has begun.) The government had seemed reluctant to intervene in any way during the first months of 1965. Perhaps the Labour government leaders were buying assent to an incomes policy, and perhaps also wage restraint seemed one element in the Stop phase of Stop-Go, against which they had inveighed so often. More probably, like most economic observers, they thought a downturn was imminent and would provide an atmosphere in which the action of the National Board could check the "cost-push" spiral.

The establishment of the Board for Prices and Incomes did not stop the spiral. The rise in retail prices from December, 1964, to June, 1965, was at an annual rate of 6.4 per cent, a higher rate than that in either 1962 or 1964 and double the rise in 1963. True, perhaps more than 1 per cent of the price increases in 1965 (or more than 2 per cent of the price increases on an annual rate) was caused by increased taxes on gasoline, cigars, cigarettes, and wines and liquors, and to the import surcharge. Nevertheless, the price rise apart from this was considerable, and its momentum was not spent. The prospect existed of wage agreements which would be announced only after they had been negotiated and agreed upon. To deny to workers gains already granted by their employers might be impossible, and to permit the *faits accomplis* would undermine the effectiveness of the National Board for Prices and Incomes, just as the National Incomes Commission's effectiveness had been aborted by the demonstration of its ineffectiveness immediately upon its creation.

Hence during July and August Mr. Brown consulted with industrialists and union leaders concerning the future of the incomes policy. In August it was reported that, pressed hard by the Chancellor of the Exchequer, Mr. Callaghan, Mr. Brown was considering recommending that an "early warning system" be made compulsory by statute so that the Board might be able to consider prospective wage settlements before they were consummated. During the last half of August Mr. Brown decided to act and to do so before the annual meeting of the Trades Union Congress scheduled for September 6. September 6 was a Monday. At a cabinet meeting held on the previous Wednesday, it was decided that the government would introduce legislation in the next session of Parliament to make advance notification of price increases and prospective wage and salary settlements compulsory. The National Board for Prices and Incomes would rule on each case, but discretion whether to refuse legal assent to increases would be in the hands of the Secretary of State for Economic Affairs.

After a day-long discussion, the General Council of the T.U.C. decided on the following day to recommend endorsement of the plan to the annual congress, on the understanding that no order would be issued under the proposed law before consultation with the T.U.C. and the Confederation of British Industry. However, before the annual congress convened the T.U.C. general secretary, Mr. George Woodcock, had conceived an alternative plan. This was that each member union should notify the T.U.C. General Council of proposed wage claims. The Council would review them and report its judgment to the union, which if it saw fit might then proceed. It was not made clear how this procedure would be related to the functioning of the National Board for Prices and Incomes.

After vigorous debate this proposal was approved on the third day of the congress, by a vote of 5,251,000 to 3,312,000. It was clear, however, that many delegates who cast supporting votes did so reluctantly, out of loyalty to two leaders for whom they had great respect and affection, Mr. Woodcock and Mr. Brown. The unions opposing were the Transport and General Workers' Union, the Electrical Trades Union, the Amalgamated Society of Boilermakers, and the National Association of Local Government Officers. Soon thereafter, however, the heads of the first three agreed to serve on the T.U.C. committee which will review proposed wage claims. Every group of unions is represented on the committee.

Employers were equally hesitant concerning the new proposal. At a meeting on September 15 the council of the new Confederation of British Industry, while expressing its distaste for the proposed system, nevertheless agreed to cooperate in it, and indeed to recommend that their members notify the government of proposed price increases even before legislation was enacted.

This was the stage of the discussions when the Labour party's annual conference was held at the end of September. Opponents of the government's policy introduced a motion opposing legislation to enforce the advance notification of wage claims. After vigorous debate, some of it dogmatic and ideological, the motion was defeated, but only by a majority of about three to two.

Later in October, the C.B.I. council discussed procedures in participation by employers. The council recommended to member firms that they should notify the government one month in advance of proposed price increases, with the provision that the notification was to be held in complete confidence unless (and until) the case was referred to the National Board for Prices and Incomes.

If a union presents a wage claim after the T.U.C. has expressed its judgment, the relevant employers' federation will notify the C.B.I. and the C.B.I. will notify the Minister of Labour at each of three stages: the presentation of the union's claim, the presentation of the employers' counteroffer, and the settlement. At any stage, the Minister of Labour may refer the case to the Secretary of State for Economic Affairs, who in turn may refer it to the National Board for Prices and Incomes.

On the day on which the C.B.I. decided to recommend this procedure to its members, the T.U.C. considered the first group of prospective wage claims. Fifty-one were submitted, thirty-six of them by the T.G.W.U. In September, the T.G.W.U. had announced that notification of claims would not be allowed to interfere with the "normal processes of collective bargaining or cause delay in the prosecution of wage claims." (Manchester *Guardian,* September 24, 1965.) As this is written, at the end of October, it is not clear whether its notification of thirty-six claims reflected a change of tactic, or whether the September statement merely implied an intention to proceed in the absence of prompt action by the T.U.C.

The T.U.C. returned all of the T.G.W.U. claims and ten of the fifteen other claims to the union presenting them, without objection. This, it was stated, did not necessarily imply full endorsement. Neither did retention of the remaining five imply disapproval; they were reserved for further information or discussion. (London *Times,* October 21, 1965.) Hence, whether the review arrangement involves more than a very loose screening is not yet clear. Perhaps only a loose screening is inevitable in the absence of screening of prices by the C.B.I. The "early warning" procedure will be executed wholly by the employers, but the involvement of the T.U.C. may give a gloss of union participation which will help to avoid the impression of one-sided restraint. In fact, of course, the restraint is not one-sided. Notification of intended price increases as well as of wage negotiations will be made.

As Parliament met at the end of October, it was not clear whether the government would submit legislation for compulsory advance notification of prospective price increases and wage claims, or would test the voluntary system for a time, depending on the pressure of opinion or other pressures to force employers not members of the C.B.I. to comply.

In obtaining the assent of the T.U.C. to the National Board for Prices and Incomes and to participation in an "early warning system," the government obtained a greater degree of assent than had ever before been obtained in peacetime to a proposed program which implies some (and perhaps a large) measure of wage restraint. The inducements by which this assent was obtained are several. First is the existence in office of the Labour government and of a Ministry of Economic Affairs headed by a trade union protagonist. It would be rash to state that the trade union leaders would fully trust any government, but at least they have a relatively high degree of trust in this Labour government. Second, by its proclamation of policies for steel nationalization and the prevention of land profiteering, among other policies, the government has sought to reassure workers of its sympathy with their social viewpoint. Although the measures for the prevention of land profiteering are moderate, a Land Commission has been created (see Chapter VIII), and while steel nationalization has been postponed until at least 1966, the policy has not been abandoned. Third, the government arranged a review of price increases parallel to the review of wage increases, and obtained the assent to it of the employers' organizations. Indeed, in the first few months of the existence of the National Board for Prices and Incomes, action against price increases was clearer and sharper than that against wage increases. In the past price increases were implicitly assumed to be largely the result of wage increases and not to need review. While the National Incomes Commission deprecated them, it did not investigate specific price increases in a way parallel to that in which it investigated wage increases. Fourth, reviews of general movements in incomes and prices are entrusted to N.E.D.C., and the trade union representatives are thereby given an official forum for the expression of their judgments concerning price movements or the distribution of incomes.

Finally, the Chancellor's April budget included a tax on capital gains and on corporate profits. Along with purely fiscal purposes and the pursuit of the government's own concepts of tax equity, it was surely hoped that these would help to convince workers that other classes are not being favored by the government.

One circumstance has been inimical to acceptance by workers of wage restraint. This is the nature of the measures adopted to meet the balance-of-payments crisis at the end of 1964. That crisis (together with the increase in old age pensions) led the government to increase certain taxes and to impose a surcharge on imports. Both actions caused some price increases. Moreover, the government imposed credit restrictions which will markedly increase the cost of housing construction. Yet in the decision by industrial workers whether to accept the new organization for wage restraint, the impact on the cost of living of the government's deflationary measures hardly weighed heavily relative to the other factors.

However, it is not at all certain that trade union leaders will accept wage decisions of the National Board for Prices and Incomes which they regard as inequitable, or whether if they do, union members will acquiesce in their acceptance. Wildcat strikes have been numerous and troublesome in Britain during recent years, and not least in 1965. They testify to widespread unrest. As a minimum, success in the incomes policy will require bringing wildcat strikes under control. From the record of events today, it seems clear that if the government moves to do so, it will move with skill and discretion. Still, the attempt may have wide repercussions. But if it is not possible for the 1965 Labour government to induce acceptance of policies that will prevent or sharply reduce wage-push inflation, with or without the ultimate test of a major strike, then it is difficult to visualize under what peacetime conditions success could be achieved. The prospects for success are discussed further in Chapter XI.

Adherence to decisions condemning price increases is also not automatically to be assumed. However, open defiance by employers is less likely than by union members. The major difficulty may turn out to be "wage drift" and corresponding changes in the prices of commodities. There are many ways of increasing both workers' incomes and the revenues from products sold, without formal changes in wage rates or prices.

VIII

Regional, Local, and Transportation Planning

While N.E.D.C. and N.I.C. were being organized, discussions of the appropriate nature of regional and local plans and planning were also proceeding. They merit brief discussion here, since an attack on regional differences in unemployment and regional problems of congestion is one aspect of the program for full employment and maximum productivity.

Although regional differences in income levels had long been noted as a problem, there had been little reason to direct special attention to them before World War II. The basic economic problem of the 1920's and 1930's had been general unemployment, and it made little difference that one region was inundated by fifteen feet of water and another by only nine. After the war, however, within the very low national average level of unemployment which prevailed during all but a few years, relatively high unemployment persisted in certain areas, and extremely high unemployment—7 to 10 per cent—in a few, notably Northern Ireland. But at the same time the Midlands and South East, and within the South East especially London, were experiencing an increasing degree of congestion. Shortages in housing and also difficulties in traffic and transport resulted, since the road network of the South was quite unsuited to handle the new traffic load.

The tendency to increasing concentration of population and production in the South is a continuing one. (For convience the term "the South" as used hereafter will include the Midlands and the South East, including London.) It is caused in minor part by the growth of population and production in the country as a whole, but beyond this by two other factors. One is the drift of industry from other regions to the South, to which much attention has been called. It results largely from the development of the use of oil and gas as fuels. This frees many industrial enterprises from dependence on coal fields and makes it advantageous for them to move closer to their major markets and to clusters of auxiliary industries. The other is the desire of individuals with rising incomes, an increasing number of whom own automobiles, to move closer to the urban amenities of London which they can now afford, to the climatically more favored areas of the country, and to the ports leading to Europe.

Industrial decline or stagnation and unemployment in other regions are the other side of the coin. Among the concomitant results has been a decline of railroad traffic in these areas.

Proposals and Actions to 1964

In spite of the relative lack of emphasis on regional problems before the war, the first government White Paper on these problems, commonly known as the Barlow Report, was published in 1938. A private organization, the Scottish Development Council, had been formed earlier, in 1931, to study the economic problems of Scotland and stimulate action on them. In 1950 the Council published the report of a committee headed by Mr. A. K. Cairncross, which emphasized the need to make relatively declining regions more attractive economically rather than merely to deter migration to other regions.[1]

The Distribution of Industry Act of 1945 designated a few large areas in Britain as "development areas" and granted certain tax advantages and financial aids to firms establishing operations within them. Before the war, a private Scottish organization had established a few "industrial estates." Under the 1945 Act, the Board of Trade was empowered to do so. These are facilities in which a building shell, power, water, transport, etc., are made ready and offered, perhaps at subsidized rates, to firms who will move in and use them.

The 1960 Local Employment Act abolished the development areas and provided instead that the benefits formerly available to these areas were to be limited to much smaller "development districts." The Board of Trade was to designate as development districts "localities in which . . . a high rate of unemployment exists, or is to be expected, and is thought likely to persist." The motive was to concentrate aid where most needed. However, this was a retrograde step, for the impact of increased employment and income extends beyond any narrowly limited area, and although a specific locality with high unemployment may not have the facilities or resources to attract an industrial venture, its establishment at a nearby favorable site may help the locality.

Attempts to control the drift to the South have been confined to limiting factory extensions of over 5,000 (1,000 since the autumn of 1965) square feet in the congested urban areas by requiring the builder to obtain an Industrial Development Certificate, and later by control of the construction of office buildings. These actions have not been highly effective in checking the drift of industry to the South East and Midland Regions as a whole.

Alongside this program, considerable emphasis was given to the establishment of "new towns" as an alternative to the growth of existing cities. Some of the new towns were merely "bedroom suburbs" rather than economic centers. While their aggregate quantitative contribution to the total problem was not great, the concept of deliberately creating new communities attracted wide attention.

A new burst of attention to regional problems occurred in 1963 when the impact of the deflationary measures of 1961 was at its maximum. In January, 1963, unemployment in the North East of England reached a postwar peak of 7.1 per cent. In that month the Prime Minister appointed Lord Hailsham minister with special responsibilities for the North East. In November in White Papers entitled *The North East* and *Central Scotland* the government published two programs for regional development and growth. A 1962 report of the Scottish Development Council (the Toothill Report) influenced the discussions going on at this time.

In mid-1963, before the White Papers had been published, the N.E.D.C. report, *Conditions Favourable to Faster Growth*, appeared. (See above, p. 47.)

The problem of regional unemployment, the report suggested, was related to that of overall growth. "A national policy of expansion," the report stated, "would improve the regional picture; and, in turn, a successful regional development programme would make it easier to achieve a national growth programme." [2]

Like all of the reports on regional problems, this one gave emphasis to inducing individuals and enterprises to remain in the declining regions rather than to expanding the facilities of the South and South East to enable those regions to receive them. It recommended attracting industry elsewhere than merely discouraging it in the South East and suggested that restrictive measures should be held to a minimum. "Success in building up industry in the slowly developing regions would mean that discouragement of expansion elsewhere could be progressively limited to areas with special problems of congestion."

The report criticized the change from the "development area" to the "development district" approach. "It is arguable that better results might be secured for the slowly expanding regions as a whole by identifying their natural growth points and seeking to attract industry to them." As positive measures, the report suggested improvement of the economic infrastructure in the relatively depressed areas and an increase in financial incentives to firms setting up operations in these areas.

A study of the problem of congestion in the South East which the government had commissioned as early as 1961 was published in March, 1964.[3] It presented a comprehensive examination of the prospective land use and housing problems of Greater London and the South East up to 1981. While the report recommended some restriction on movement of industry to the South East, like the N.E.D.C. report is stressed increasing the attractions of the other parts of the country. One program suggested to alleviate the problems of London was "a fresh and much larger program of new and expanded towns, the individual expansion scheme being on a bigger scale than those in the current programme," and these towns to be located well away from London.[4]

The government's actions in 1963 and 1964 were consistent with these doctrines. A growth zone was identified in the North East and four growth areas in Central Scotland where efforts to induce industrial expansion were to be concentrated. The government announced that special attention would be paid to improving communications within the North East growth zone and between that zone and the rest of the country. Town center redevelopment and general urban improvement were also to receive high priority. A similar program for increased public investment "to modernise the infrastructure services" was outlined for Central Scotland. It was announced that facilities in both regions for industrial training of school-leavers and adults would be increased. The government also issued assurances designed to allay fears about the instability of government policy and announced increases in the financial incentives offered.

Meanwhile, an attack had also been made on traffic congestion. The construction of a number of limited-access motorways begun in the 1950's and continuing redesign of London's traffic controls and routes, which has been emphasized more recently, are intended to meet the traffic problem. Both have accomplished some improvement, but between some cities the improvement in intercity roads has served mainly to keep the congestion from increasing as rapidly as it would have otherwise. On the other hand, in spite of the absence of any machinery for systematic evaluation of the services of the nationalized industries, the growing deficit of the railways attracted such attention that finally Dr. Richard Beeching was drawn from Imperial Chemical Industries, Ltd., appointed as railway "tsar," and asked to plan and execute the elimination of superfluous railway facilities. Dr. Beeching set about the job with vigor, and in 1963 and 1964 terminated service on a number of branch lines.

Late in 1963 the report to the Ministry of Transport of a commission headed by Professor Colin Buchanan attracted wide attention. (*Traffic in Towns* [Reports of the Steering Group and Working Group Appointed by the Minister of Transport], London: H.M.S.O., 1963.) The report denounced in sweeping terms the existing approach to regional and local planning. Present piecemeal measures attacking detailed problems as they appear, the report stated, are permitting the automobile to encroach steadily on the amenities available to the public. It called for immediate, comprehensive, long-run planning of cities and of the entire country's space to design a future living complex instead of letting it develop at random.

Following the publication of the Buchanan report, it was announced in May, 1964, that a group had been set up to advise on "the techniques, procedures and machinery of town and country planning" in the light of "major developments that lie ahead in the planning field." It was thought that in addition to considering such subjects as urban renewal and road planning the group would study the relationship of local land plans to regional plans. The function of the group was to advise departments of the Ministry of Housing and Local Government. The first report of this Planning Advisory Group, which appeared in 1965, recommended area action plans to supplement local plans.

These actions and proposals signified a substantial shift of initiative and responsibility from local authorities to the central government. Regional planning and within it much local planning was to be done neither by local authorities nor by regional authorities created for the purpose, but by the central government. Since any regional plan affects the entire country and should be drawn up with a view to the national effect, this shift of authority was inevitable. However, since the approval of local planning bodies and councils was required for many measures of zoning and land use, they were still able to block actions of many types to which there was strong local objection.

The recognition of regional problems raised the question of restructuring governmental machinery to administer measures with specific regional applications. The Minister of Housing and Local Government in March, 1964, referred to the need "for strong regional arms of central government," and added, "That is what we are providing." (Manchester *Guardian,* March 7, 1964.) For the North East it was announced that the offices of the government departments mainly concerned with the program would be brought together in a single building in Newcastle and their work would be closely coordinated, but by the time the Conservative government fell in October, no such groupings of regional offices had actually been carried out. Regional offices already existed in Scotland.

LABOUR GOVERNMENT POLICIES

With regard to some aspects of regional and local planning, the differences between the two major parties were ones of emphasis; with regard to other aspects, something more.

The Labour government took a new tack with respect to nationalizing the transportation system. The trade unions, especially the National Union of Railwaymen, had objected vigorously to the closing of uneconomic railway lines without an analysis of all means of transport. One of the Labour party's election pledges had been to make such an analysis. When the new government took office, it asked Dr. Beeching to conduct this more comprehensive study, but after some controversy about the conditions of the study he declined. The government then appointed Lord Hinton, former executive in atomic energy research and in the electricity industry, to direct a study of all transport facilities and recommend long-run plans to the Minister of Transport. Like Beeching, Lord Hinton is highly respected as both competent and resistant to political considerations.

The new government undertook to do what the Conservative government had delayed attempting—to overcome the resistance of the National Union of Railwaymen to the introduction of "liner trains" with "open terminals." Liner trains are proposed freight trains which would travel at high speed between major cities without intermediate stops, carrying goods prepacked in standardized containers. At the present time all collection and delivery of freight hauled on the railways is by British Railway trucks. It was judged by Dr. Beeching that the liner train proposal would not succeed unless the terminals were opened to private truckers. The Railwaymen have strongly opposed opening them. During the summer of 1965 opposition from a contrasting source appeared. Whereas the Railwaymen objected to the loss of local hauling to private truckers, private truckers objected to the loss of intercity hauling to the railways. Mr. Tom Fraser, the Minister of Transport under the Labour government, has consistently expressed both the firm intention of proceeding with the scheme and his expectation of union cooperation. Before this essay is in print, the issue will have been settled by the inauguration of the service or evaded by its postponement.

The rapid development of growing areas has been accompanied both by what Labour party speakers have referred to as "anarchy" in the determination of land use and by a widespread sense of injustice at the great gains obtained by fortunate or shrewd land owners. After studying for almost a year how it should meet these problems, the Labour government announced in September, 1965, in a White Paper on the Land Commission (Cmnd. 2771) a proposal "to secure that the right land is available at the right time for the implementation of national, regional, and local plans," and "to secure that a substantial part of the development value created by the community returns to the community, and that the burden of the cost of land for essential purposes is reduced."

During the election campaign the Labour party had emphasized its intention of preventing land profiteering. Various Labour speakers came close to pledging as the means to this end the nationalization of land to be developed. Many dispassionate observers rightly feared that the prospect, and later the fact of nationalization, if it became a fact, would markedly retard not only private housing construction in the areas most in need of added housing but also other economic development. The White Paper relieved this fear, for the measure announced to prevent (or lessen) profiteering was simply a levy on the increase in land value accruing because of development. (Since the increase in value typically follows administrative action by planning authorities which makes development possible, identification of the relevant increase in value is somewhat less difficult than might be supposed.) The rate of levy, effective on the day the White Paper was issued, was 40 per cent. It was to be increased "at reasonably short intervals" to 45 and then 50 per cent. Thereafter, the Land Commission to be created would consider further increases.

The prospect of increases in the rate will presumably accelerate land sale and development in the interval. Gains subject to the levy will not be subject to the capital gains tax which is one component of the Labour government's new tax measures, or to profits tax. Since the capital gains tax rate is set at 30 per cent and the rate of corporation tax may be 40 per cent, the increase in tax burden effected by the levy on development value is very moderate. There will be two major difficulties in administration of the measure, the inherent difficulty of establishing the valuation to be used as the base for calculating the increase due to development and the shortage of trained assessors. The later may be overcome by a "crash" training program.

To achieve the other goals announced in the White Paper, the government announced its intention to introduce legislation for the creation of a Land Commission. The Commission will be empowered to buy, in the market or by compulsory purchase, land deemed necessary for housing or other development purposes and to sell it to local authorities, housing associations, cooperative groups, or private builders. Sale to the first three groups may be at less than the market value.

This aspect of the proposal is subject to two criticisms. The planning functions of the commission duplicate functions already assigned to local authorities and regional development authorities; the duplication may retard action. Also, the sale of land below market value may cause land to be used for housing which is so scarce that the city and region would be better served if it were allocated to other uses. However, relationships may be worked out by which the commission will be a useful operating agent. Establishment of the commission has the virtue of satisfying a widespread emotional demand for public action. Its establishment may have been necessary to make the moderate levy on capital gains palatable. (The Labour government of the immediate postwar years imposed a tax of 100 per cent.) The legislation marks a retreat, or an advance, from dogma to common sense, or, one might say, marks the elevation of social welfare above social justice, and in comparison with the alternatives open to the government should be regarded as facilitating development rather than interfering with it.

Soon after it took office, the new government had announced its intention to relieve congestion by speeding up the establishment of added new towns in various areas. Plans for a large new town at Leyland/Chorley in Lancashire were announced in mid-1965 and new towns for other areas were being considered. This conversion of erstwhile rural or suburban land to town use is of course the cause of especially large increases in land value, resulting from administrative decision concerning the location of a new town. The development value levy will reduce the private gains which result.

During the 1964 election campaign, the leaders of the Labour party had denounced the "Tory freedom" which had created two nations, an overcongested South and a starved North, and had announced that to replace the Conservative *ad hoc* attack on regional planning, if elected, they would institute regional planning and regional administration for every region of the country. When the new government had been organized, the Department of Economic Affairs set itself vigorously to the administrative task.

In December, Mr. Brown announced the division of England other than the South East into six regions for regional planning purposes. Scotland and Wales were also to be regarded as regions for the purpose. Pending a review of the policies stated in the White Paper on the South East, decision concerning regional organization there was withheld. In each region an economic planning board and an economic planning council would be created. Each board, headed by an official of the Department of Economic Affairs of the rank of Under-Secretary, would consist of regional representatives of other ministries and would be concerned with coordinating the work of government departments within the region. The councils would be advisory and would consist about equally of local government officials, representatives of employers, and representatives of the trade unions, plus a few academic experts.

Each planning board was to sit in a major city of its region and as soon as possible the regional staffs of all of the ministries were to be gathered together in the same city. In February, 1965, the first such regional office was opened in Manchester.

To foster the revival of the declining regions the government used with increased vigor the tool of industrial estates, now termed "advance factories." In November, 1964, the Board of Trade announced a program for the construction of twenty-nine advance factories in development areas and in September, 1965, when all of the twenty-nine were under construction (and some were let), announced plans for twenty-six more, twelve of them in Scotland. While the earlier industrial estates have attracted only certain types of light and fairly "footloose" industry and give little evidence of becoming foci of further development, they have been fairly quickly occupied. Presumably the same will be true of the new advance factories.

ARE THESE THE RIGHT POLICIES?

The difficulty of inducing economic expansion in a relatively depressed area has frequently been underestimated, as has been shown by experience to date in England and elsewhere. Fiscal and financial inducements, plus improvement in infrastructure, often fail to have the expected effect since the factors determining the most advantageous location for a firm are extremely complex. The number of truly "footloose" industries, which can economically locate in almost any place that is made attractive by tax and other financial inducements, is far fewer than appears on the surface. Neither closeness to market, closeness to raw materials, closeness to labor, nor these in combination, even given the existence of adequate and convenient infrastructure, are always the major determinants of location. Often the availability of a number of auxiliary services—research, specialized services or expert advice of various kinds, nearness of a foundry, of a precision machine shop, etc.—is of quite unexpected importance, and many of these services in turn have no inducement to move to an area unless a number of customers are simultaneously available.

Thus a problem which appears on the surface to be merely one of financial and other inducements to a single firm or a small group of obviously related firms turns out instead to be an "ecological" one. It is impossible to identify an effective industrial complex and establish it at one stroke; and while there are some enterprises which can be attracted in the absence of others whose presence in turn will make the area more attractive to others, the technical knowledge by which to determine feasible sequences is typically simply not in existence. Also, the relocation of offices involves more complex considerations than are sometimes apparent. There often are basic reasons (sometimes not fully realized by a firm itself until it considers the consequences of moving) for the location of a company's offices in a certain city, even though a congested one. Of course, the government can make almost any area attractive to industry if it provides sufficiently great open or hidden subsidies. But the economic cost of achieving the revival of some depressed areas may be much greater than anticipated.

There are also hidden costs of preventing the drift to the South East, just as there are hidden costs of permitting it. There is a drift of industry to the South East and to existing cities because in changed technical conditions production can be carried on there at reduced cost. And there is a drift of population not merely because of loss of jobs in the declining regions but also because, jobs being equal, many persons prefer living in the South Eeast, in or near the cities, and near the Continent. On the other hand, the drift is partly due to the fact that the industrial plants and social capital of the declining regions, having been constructed in the nineteenth century for industries employing nineteenth-century methods, are simply obsolete, and now unattractive. If some of the areas were starting from a blank slate, they would probably be more attractive to industry than they are now. Where this is true, the probability is greater that it is economic for the government to bear the cost of change which will induce new activity.

It is not certain, therefore, to what degree the policy of maintaining declining regions should, ideally, be carried. Two questions are involved. Will the persons whose livelihood in declining regions is disappearing, and their descendants, be happier in those areas or in the South East? (The senior author of this essay has noted with some amusement that many of the intellectuals who argue vigorously for the prevention of further congestion in the South East were born in other regions but have chosen to live in London.) And, will the financial and social cost to the rest of the population of providing the inducements needed to make uneconomic locations economic to individual firms be greater or less than the financial and social costs of meeting the problems of increased population density in the South East?

Actual policy will be a compromise; to some degree movement to the South East will occur; to some degree it will be prevented. Policies to date have not been based on explicit consideration of the counterbalancing costs, and the counterbalancing happiness and unhappiness. Rather, it has been assumed without analysis that increased concentration of population is undesirable. However, as judged by the caution in a statement here and there in the relevant chapter (Chapter 8) of the *National Plan,* the government may now be proceeding with more awareness of the complexity of the problem.

No dogmatic statement concerning what specific course of action would be best is justified, partly because no precise or even approximate measurement of the alternative social costs is possible. However, whatever the proportions in which it is decided to aid growing regions to receive people and on the other hand to provide inducements in declining regions to hold people there, sensibly planned and administered measures by the government will advance social welfare greatly as compared with taking no bold action at all. For the decay on the one hand and congestion on the other resulting from private actions alone must be attacked boldly, even though the action may turn out not to have been the ideal one.

IX

Planning in France: A Frame
of Reference[1]

In the discussions in the press and on radio and television during the period of formation of N.E.D.C., there had been frequent references to French planning as providing a model which Britain might well follow. When N.E.D.C. came into being there were some Britons who thought that in N.E.D.C. an institution had been created by which Britain might hope to achieve some of the successes attributed to French planning. During the period of the new Labour government, on the other hand, there have been virtually no references in the press to French planning, and yet for the first time in some of its aspects Britain's planning machinery is coming to resemble that in France. It will be useful to summarize French planning procedures here as a point of departure for evaluation of the institutions which have been developing in Britain.

The feature of French planning most stressed in British discussions—indeed, the only feature which received much stress—was the forecasting of potential output, in the aggregate and by industry groups, for a few years in the future, and of the investment necessary during the intervening years to attain it. This vision of the available future market and the path to it, a vision arrived at cooperatively by government and industry, was taken as the central feature of French planning. Execution of the plan was thought of as essentially spontaneous. In part, this misunderstanding was a result of less attention by French officials, in explaining their planning procedure, to the execution of the plan than to its formulation. However, since the P.E.P. report, *Growth in the British Economy,*

101

published in 1960, presents a very general and very brief but entirely accurate summary of the methods of executing the plan, it is obvious that they were ignored partly because it suited the temper of the times to ignore them.

French planning methods have been modified progressively from 1946 to the present time, and indeed are still undergoing change. The modifications, however, relate mainly to the scope of the plan and the method of formulating it, rather than to its execution. The first plan, for the years 1947 to 1950, related solely to three public and three private industries in which rapid reconstruction was essential, and set production targets for only the three private ones—steel, cement, and farm machinery. When the plan was extended through 1952 to include the entire period of the Marshall Plan, fuels and fertilizers were added. The second plan, covering 1954 to 1957, included tentative accounts for the economy as a whole, and set production targets for the economy as a whole, and for each sector. By the time of the third plan, for the years 1958 to 1961, the entire economy was analyzed systematically with interlocking estimates (input-output estimates) for the various sectors. The discussion below applies primarily to the period of formulation and execution of this third plan, the period when French planning attracted great attention in Britain and influenced the formation of N.E.D.C.

FORMULATING THE PLAN

The central planning body in France is the *Commissariat Général du Plan de Modernisation et d'Équipement* or General Planning Commission, usually referred to as the *Commissariat au Plan*. (Perhaps for the sake of euphony, in common usage the *du* has been replaced by *au*.) By law all plans which the *Commissariat au Plan* formulates must be submitted for examination to the Economic and Social Council (formerly, the Economic Council), a body of more than 160 members all but a few of whom represent economic interest groups.[2] But each of the first three plans was presented to the Council only after it had been completed and announced. The *Commissariat au Plan* is an "independent" body only in the sense that it is nonpolitical. All of its members are either civil servants drawn from other agencies or experts employed for the purpose, and its director is a high-level government official, with ready access to General De Gaulle.

The contact of the *Commissariat au Plan* with industry, including nationalized industry, and with the social services of the government in the formulation of each plan is through *Commissions de Modernisation* or "planning commissions" and, under them, working parties. These include representatives of the *Commissariat au Plan* and of the industry group involved. In the formulation of the third plan there were seventeen commissions; for the fourth plan, twenty-two. In addition, "horizontal commissions" carry out the integrated analysis of basic economic factors or functions. Those for the fourth plan were General Economic and Financial, Manpower, Productivity, Scientific and Technical Research, and Regional Plans.

The locus of power in the vertical commissions and working parties is accurately indicated by their composition. Of the more than 3,100 members during the formulation of the fourth plan, fully 47 per cent were either civil servants or independent experts appointed by the government, 41 per cent were representatives of employers (including the nationalized industries) or employers' associations, only 9 per cent were trade unionists, and 3 per cent were representatives of farm groups. Union representation was low partly because many unions feared that planning would run counter to their interests and refused to join the activity. In any event, government officials and experts, plus representatives of employers, dominate, in decisions as well as in numbers, and trade unions have a very small voice. The industry representatives then as well as in the formulation of other plans were not representatives of the rank and file. They represented the important interest groups, it is true, but typically they were spokesmen of the more innovational sectors of their industries. As evidence of the domination of the commissions and working parties by individuals not representing private economic interests, either the chairman or the vice chairman of all but one of the twenty-seven commissions existing in 1963 was a civil servant, and in most of them the *rapporteur* who reported the commission's work to the *Commissariat au Plan* was one as well.[3]

In the case of each plan, planning began with a preliminary estimate of the rate of growth which might be achieved and with a government directive to the *Commissariat au Plan* concerning the main objectives of the plan. In the third plan the target growth rate was 5 per cent per year, and the major goals were growth and restoration of a favorable balance of payments. The *Commissariat* then prepared tentative estimates of the possible rate of increase in productivity in each sector of the economy and of the production which the sector might contribute to the anticipated 1961 total, the investment which would be needed in each sector, the labor requirements for each sector, imports which would be required for the production indicated, the exports needed to attain the balance-of-payments goal, and so on. The vertical commissions and working parties plus the horizontal commissions then went into a long process of revising these estimates, evaluating the consistency or inconsistency of the targets for each industry, revising them, and reevaluating, until finally, some three years after the process began, a document presenting a consistent overall plan was produced.[4]

The final plan was submitted to the parliament. As in the case of the previous plans, in its preoccupation with political matters the parliament gave the plan only cursory attention, thus leaving the planners a free hand.

The forecasts of increase in productivity during the plan period, like those of each previous and later plan, were not based on the assumption merely of reaction by the existing range of firms to the levels of demand indicated for 1961. They were judgments of what could be accomplished if the more progressive firms in each industry were given full scope to advance, and if their advancing level of productivity became more widespread in the industry, perhaps by these firms themselves taking over more of the industry.

The plan did not include an incomes policy. The plan was formulated in constant prices, not because these were forecast, but because the behavior of prices was regarded as outside the scope of the preparation of the plan. It was obvious, however, that price rises could not be ignored. The pressure for expansion during the two previous plan periods had been accompanied by a continuing rise in prices. Further continuance of this inflation would cause greater difficulties now that the Common Market was about to begin operations on January 1, 1959, and France would be required to meet the competition of its fellow members. One conclusion had been reached very early in the planning process: the required level of exports could not be reached, nor imports held down to the forecast level, except by drastic action. The plan nevertheless assumed a gradual corrective process and the attainment of a favorable balance of payments over a six-year period.

However, an advisory committee of experts (headed by Jacques Rueff, who had little faith in planning) had been appointed to recommend a solution to the problems caused by the upward price trend. The committee recommended devaluation of the franc and thereafter a deflationary credit policy. The political upheavals of 1957 and 1958 delayed action on these recommendations, but by the end of 1958 De Gaulle, who had come to power in May, had turned his attention to them and had accepted them. Although the exchange rate had already been allowed to fall sharply in the autumn of 1957, at the end of 1958 a further devaluation of 17½ per cent (or to 40 per cent below the July 1957 rate) was announced, and in 1959 deflationary fiscal and credit policies were in force. The annual increase in output fell to 1 per cent, but the balance of payments reached equilibrium in nine months. Thereafter, in 1960 and 1961, the rate of increase in output again rose. Price rises also reappeared; French planning has been no more able than planning elsewhere to arrive at an incomes policy which would prevent them.

EXECUTING THE PLAN: "ACTIVE" PLANNING

On approval of the plan, comprehensive and vigorous intervention by the government began, to see that the targets were attained. Or rather, the intervention under the preceding plans continued. French planning, M. Pierre Massé, the present director of the *Commissariat au Plan* has said, is "more than indicative and less than imperative." The phrases are correct, but how much more than indicative, even though also much less than imperative, is the actual process! In M. Massé's delicate Gallic phraseology in another place, "the heart of the matter is that French planning is active; it . . . regulates the stimuli and aids at the disposal of the public departments in such a manner that the objectives assigned to the private sector are achieved.[5]

The execution of the plan begins in the nationalized sector. This includes coal, electricity and atomic energy, and gas; railway and major air transport; telephone and telegraph; aircraft construction;

the Renault automobile company; control of the two ocean shipping companies through joint ownership; and leadership in advance in the oil industry, also through joint ownership. The governmentally appointed managers of all these companies have taken part in the formulation of the plan, and a part of the completed plan is an agreement between the *Commissariat au Plan* and each nationalized company that will need financing. The agreement relates to the increase in the company's output, the general nature of its advances in technology, and the prices it will charge. In return for assurances concerning these matters, the *Fonds de Développement Économique et Social* enters into a firm agreement, to be discussed below, that the necessary finance will be provided. However, government companies not needing financing have not been docilely obedient to the plan. Occasionally, they have expanded in disregard of the plan. (Renault was a leader in offering wage increases and an increase in vacations opposed by the government.)

Incentives had been offered to private firms in each plan. In general, however, not until the fourth plan were they offered explicitly for the purpose of accelerating the rate of increase in productivity. Rather, they were offered to increase the production of a type of output for which the plan indicated a need. Thus, in the third plan, when the need for a large increase in exports was emphasized, special financial rewards were offered to any firm which achieved the export of more than 20 per cent of its output (and whose exports exceeded a small minimum value).

Implicitly, however, emphasis always centered on increase in productivity. An important element in the regulation of "stimuli and aids . . . in such a manner that the objectives assigned to the private sector are achieved" is consensus among a network of government officials concerning the actions to be taken, and complete readiness on their part to discriminate among firms. They selected efficient and innovational ones as chosen instruments, and on occasion not only permitted but encouraged them to drive their inefficient small competitors out of business so that the average level of productivity should rise. Shonfield cites the "undisguised glee" with which a member of the staff of the *Commissariat au Plan* described the "vrai holocauste" which was being wrought among the small, backward firms in a certain industry.[6]

In part, then, the difference between the rates of British and

French advance in productivity has been due not to the greater innovational tendency and energy of French managers (which may also exist) but to the fact that the more innovational managers have not only been given free rein, but aided. Shonfield notes also the presence of an 80-20 rule of thumb. Where 20 per cent of the firms in a manufacturing industry produce less than 80 per cent of the output of the industry, the staff of the *Commissariat au Plan* tends to regard the industry as inefficient and to look with favor both on mergers if there appears to be any technical advantage in them and on price and other policies which will drive the inefficient firms out of business.[7] The French response to the screams of outrage of trade unions, small employers, and individuals losing their jobs, has been to provide generous termination pay and aid in retraining and finding another job. It is of course pertinent that French unions except in certain industries are weaker than the British ones, and that less than 10 per cent of the members of the planning commissions and working parties were union representatives.

The means by which control has been exercised in the private sector is, first (and least important), direct government provision of finance. The governmental *Fonds de Développement Économique et Social* or Economic and Social Development Fund, a "holding company" for a number of government investment institutions established at various times in the past, has available large amounts of funds. In 1960, in addition to financing approved investments of the nationalized industries for which they had neither internal funds nor budget funds and making a fairly large amount of loans in agriculture, it made loans to private nonagricultural business borrowers which constituted 8 per cent of their external financing throughout the successive plan periods.[8] Its loans to nationalized industries have been only for projects which were a part of the plan, and its loans to private borrowers for projects consistent with the plan.

A second set of relevant activities are those of the *Caisse des Dépôts et des Consignations*. Along with other minor sources of funds, the *Caisse* receives all money deposited in the savings department of the post office and all surplus funds of the private savings banks, all of the pension funds of the nationalized industries and local authorities, and all government tax revenues pending their expenditure. The sum total makes it by far the largest bank in

France its resources equal the total current (in American usage, "demand") deposits of all private French banks. It uses them in the bond and medium-term credit market. It is very important in the medium-term loan market and dominates the Paris bond market, its support for an issue more or less assuring its success. While the *Caisse* is independent of political control, its president is a senior official of the Ministry of Finance, and indeed during the 1950's and early 1960's has been an official who aided in the development of French planning machinery. Under his guidance, the *Caisse* has directed its loans and its bond purchases to firms who desired the funds for projects consistent with the plan. In view of the huge size of the *Caisse*, this policy must have exerted great influence.

Next among the more important credit control levers is the semigovernmental *Crédit* National, a "bankers' bank." The *Crédit National* stands ready to purchase from commercial banks medium-term loans of up to five years exceeding one million francs and longer-term bonds exceeding 2,500,000 francs provided it has approved the loan as bond issue in advance. Its assurance that it will purchase in turn requires assurance from the *Banque de France* that it will buy the paper in question from *Crédit National* if desired. The requirements for purchase by the *Banque de France* contain no reference to the *Commissariat au Plan,* but so completely is the approval of the *Commissariat* a part of the process that the *Crédit National* advises prospective users of its services to obtain the endorsement of the *Commissariat* before coming to it for approval of a prospective loan.

Finally, a firm so well established that its own securities will find a ready market does not escape the net. Any new issue of shares or debentures exceeding one million francs (and almost any smaller issue is too costly to be practical) requires approval by the Treasury (which is within the Ministry of Finance). And the Treasury approves issues only on the advice of the *Commissariat au Plan.*

The quantitative significance of these instruments is as follows. During the four years of the third plan, 1958–61, public funds financed one-fourth of all fixed investment in France, the issue of shares and loans on the capital market financed almost 12 per cent, and medium-term credit plus loans by specialized financial organizations financed about 23 per cent. Of this 23 per cent, governmental agencies or closely associated agencies (as described above) controlled more than one-half. Thus the government held in its hands the means of controlling about one-half of all financing of fixed investment, which means very much more than one-half of all externally financed investment.[9]

In short, under French planning a very large sector of the money market is an instrument of the planners. A network of government officials, having worked out with the more innovational producers of France an allocation which they believe will best serve the purposes of economic growth in France, uses a network of institutions to push the allocation of funds in the direction desired. Their influence should not be exaggerated. Even during the period of the third plan, one-half of all fixed investment was financed from sources not under the control of the planning network, and this percentage has increased in subsequent years. Moreover, certainly a large part of the financing by the governmentally controlled institutions would have gone on precisely as it did even if the plan had not existed. Also, investment in increased stocks of goods is undoubtedly financed from internal funds to a much greater extent than is fixed investment. Thereby, decisions to expand production within the limits of existing capacity are far less under the influence of the planners than are decisions to expand plant capacity. But with maximum allowance for these qualifications, the degree of control by the planning network over the allocation of investment is impressive.

While the credit controls are central in the mechanism for executing each plan, there are also other controls. For example, mergers, to which large private firms are seldom averse, can be made only with government approval. Also, the administration of the tax laws is important. Here, as in the allocation of investment funds, the French do not shrink from administrative discrimination if it is deemed in the public interest. Thus, by law there are a number of categories of tax relief which may be granted to individual private enterprises for specified reasons; the text of the fourth plan lists eight of them which economic planners can employ. The authorities may enter into actual contracts by which "a specific advantage is accorded to an enterprise as a counterpart of a programme of investment which is judged to be of interest." [10]

As examples of what has been done: under the third plan firms exporting at least 20 per cent of their turnover, if that 20 per cent equals 50,000 francs or more, received very favorable depreciation provisions and also the right to have their problems considered by a special commission representing the *Commissariat au Plan* and the Ministry of Finance. Firms whose increase in capital was approved by the *Commissariat au Plan* were authorized to deduct from their profits tax liability for each of seven years 5 per cent of the increase. Perhaps most interesting was an inducement offered to retail shops to persuade them to keep prices down. One method of assessing taxes, where precise net income is difficult to establish to the satisfaction of the tax authorities, is to apply to an estimate of the firm's turnover a standard ratio of the margin of profit assumed to be normal in that type of business. In 1963 retail firms who agreed to maintain prices recommended by the Price Control Office were in return given a guarantee against any increase from the previous year in the estimate of their turnover.[11] The French planners, it is obvious, are far from holding the private market sacrosanct and have effective instruments for intervening in it.

The *Commissariat au Plan* has not sought to dominate other agencies. It has succeeded because there exists throughout the government a network of officials who have come to believe deeply in the type of planning being done. The *Commissariat* brings them together; they reach a consensus on what should be done; then, rather spontaneously, they act in concert to move the appropriate levers. While outside the government the sanctions described above constitute a power system, within the government French planning is very much indicative, not imperative.

EVALUATION

There is no clear evidence that the difference between France and Britain in postwar economic performance is due primarily to French planning. Indeed, this may be a minor factor. The French Ministry of Labor stated in 1951 that the top hiring age for middle-rank executives (*cadres*), which had been sixty years in 1898, declined to fifty in 1945, forty-five in 1950, and forty in 1951.[12] The indicated drop within a period of a single year is cause to suspect the precision of the figures, but there is no reason to question the trend they indicate. It suggests a profound change, accelerating after World War II, in the attitude toward management. This

change may be a reflection of factors which are the most fundamental cause of the improved French performance.

Thus, planning may not be the most important cause of the
improved performance. Moreover, the actions taken may be building up troubles for the future. The planning procedure encourages
the cartelization of industry. Up to the present time, the dominant
firms in each industry have acted to accelerate technical progress,
but rigidities are being created which would permit future executives with different attitudes to rely on monopolistic arrangements
rather than innovational vigor for the maintenance of the positions
of their companies.

A further criticism of French planning, at least from the viewpoint of some observers, is that the successive plans have not been
democratically arrived at, at least until the fourth plan. Rather,
planning has been a "conspiracy in the public interest" (Shonfield's
phrase). The present Commissaire Général, M. Pierre Massé, has
moved both to acquaint the political bodies more fully concerning
the implications of each plan before its final formulation and to
reach a consensus on incomes policy. There is no need to evaluate
his move toward "democratization" here. However, it may be noted
that up to the present his attempt to attain consensus on an incomes
policy has not succeeded. This is not necessarily a defect of French
planning, but it is an indication that that planning has been no more
successful in this respect than has the British variety.

No overall appraisal of French planning need be attempted
here. This summary of its operation, with the reflections to which it
naturally leads one concerning the differences in institutions in the
two countries, provides a convenient framework against which to
examine the evolution of British planning machinery.

British Planning and British Character

Between 1946 and 1958, while France was developing her planning institutions step by step, Britain was progressively withdrawing from active intervention in the control of production or of the market, except for fiscal and monetary measures to regulate the level of aggregate consumption and investment. When she then reversed her course in 1961 and considered the establishment of new planning institutions, her leaders talked now and then of French institutions as a model, yet the institutions she evolved between 1961 and 1964 only remotely resemble those in France. In 1965 the resemblance has increased. The facts of the institutional evolution in Britain and France have been sketched above. A brief discussion of the significance of the British institutions may be introduced by considering the reasons for the divergence and now convergence between Britain and France.

DIFFERENCES BETWEEN FRENCH AND BRITISH PLANNING INSTITUTIONS

The discussion may take as a point of departure a summary of three major differences between French planning machinery and British planning machinery as it exists in late 1965. One concerns the nature of the relationship between the government planners— for in Britain too the planning agency is now a government body— and private bodies. The role remaining to N.E.D.C. after the transfer of central responsibility for planning to the Department of Economic Affairs is not closely comparable to the role in France of the Economic and Social Council. For that large council, even in its new somewhat enlarged role, will meet perhaps once every two years, or at most once every year, to receive and criticize proposals of the *Commissariat au Plan*. The government would like its approval, but can do without it. The important contact with employers in France is through the *Commissions de Modernisations* and the working parties, and these are groups of like-minded men, some within and some outside of government, working toward common ends.

In Britain, however, no matter how influential the Department of Economic Affairs may become in the formation of additional "little Neddies," the "little Neddies" are constituted largely of individuals who are self-consciously representatives of economic interest groups. So also is N.E.D.C. itself. Everyone concerned now recognizes that, like the T.U.C. members, the employer members represent organizations. The parallelism between the trade union and employer representation on N.E.D.C. is not complete, for in large measure the employer members and the groups of men for whom they speak control the organizations they lead, whereas in much greater degree the T.U.C. leaders are the servants of the attitudes of the members of the unions which compose the T.U.C. But that the employer and trade union members of N.E.D.C. all represent economic interest groups is recognized. Of course there are economic interest groups in France as well, but they are far more fractionated in France than in Britain, far more accustomed to being at loggerheads with each other, and far more resigned to having the government break the deadlock among them and act without explicitly bargaining with them.

Government officials of Britain do not, as in France, collude with selected industrialists in what the officials and the industrialists agree is the public interest. Rather, the government negotiates with representatives of private associations, at arm's length, and those private associations include powerful labor unions as well as groups of industrialists.

The second difference concerns the status of the central planning agency. The *Commissariat au Plan* is an apolitical body. It survived without change in leadership or function the shift from the Fourth Republic to De Gaulle. Each of the three successive *Commissaires Générals* came to it not from political office but from business management. The present one, Pierre Massé, had been a very successful head of the French nationalized electricity industry. None of the three had ministerial pretensions. In its relationships within the government, the *Commissariat au Plan* did not establish a new focus or layer of authority; it became the means by which the visions of a group of devoted men throughout the government could be made real.

In Britain, framing a plan will also require unity of viewpoint or mutual accommodation among officials in many departments, for example the Treasury, the Board of Trade, and the Ministries of Labour, of Housing and Local Government, of Public Building and Works, of Science and Education, and of Technology, to mention only a few. But the mutual accommodation will have to be arranged, not by an unobtrusive apolitical body, but a powerful department whose actions will in some degree be an infringement on the spheres of other departments, no matter how cordial the relationships among the ministers may be.

Lastly, there are basic differences in the means of implementation in the two countries. There is no tradition in Britain of quasi-governmental supervision of bank loans, discretionary governmental control over issues of corporate securities, or the discriminatory application of tax laws between enterprises whose actions are consistent with the economic plan and those whose actions are not. The government's present powers of discriminatory inducement are limited to its roles as purchaser, lender, or grantor. These may seem formidable enough, but they lack the flexibility and the comprehensiveness of the French control over access to the private financial market and the French tradition of discretionary discrimination in taxation. At least superficially, because of its weaker instruments the task of the British government in effectuating a plan is far more difficult than that of the government of France.

How have the differences come about? This question will be a useful introduction to an appraisal of developments in Britain.

Social Origins of the Differences

In the most general terms, the reason is that the planning machinery of each country grew out of the country's social institutions, and the two sets of social institutions were radically different.

France: Paternalism in a Stalemate Society

A tendency to find no effective solution to national problems except through (limited) centralized and somewhat paternalistic control has pervaded French life, and still does. In the political field particularistic groups held rigidly to their conflicting dogmas. Their leaders refused—indeed because of their attitudes they were unable—to reach mutual accommodation. As a result, when action was needed it had to be imposed by a central authority which superseded the legislature. The intransigent groups were thereby relieved of facing the consequences of their rigidity. What is more, they were relieved of the necessity of taking action—of facing problems, making decisions, and bearing responsibility for the results. Rigid adherence to dogma is, in one aspect, a means of avoiding responsibility for practical action, and it has certainly been so in the French case.

From the Revolution to 1870, in successive swings which are familiar even to casual students of French history, either parliaments were paralyzed by futile squabbling among groups each holding to its inflexible view of what was right, or one evanescent coalition of expediency followed another; then, when the country became frustrated at the squabbling, the parliament yielded power to rulers the nation permitted to be authoritarian within limits. It is not necessary to cite the historical details; it will be sufficient to remind the reader that, unlike Britain and America, France does not refer simply to its republic. It refers to the First Republic, the Second, the Third, the Fourth, and now finally the Fifth Republic. Each of the previous ones broke down in one or the other of the ways mentioned.

After 1878, when for more than fifty years there was no acute peacetime crisis, the country could afford hamstrung parliaments, and government by deals among splinter groups worked after a fashion. A political scientist has termed the Third and Fourth Republics (or, more precisely, within them the period 1878–1934) the "stalemate society." [1] Stalemate among particularistic groups was adequate during peacetime for seventy years, but in the crises after World War II it again became intolerable, and De Gaulle assumed power—the latest version of a phenomenon which has occurred now and again since Napoleon. (Over the entire period since the French Revolution, there has been development in political institutions; the political structure was not static, but there is no need here to consider the nuances of development.)

The avoidance of responsibility for practical action, which has been one cause of such action in the political field, has been a cause of somewhat parallel developments in financial institutions. During the eighteenth century the development in France of modern banking practices and of nongovernment credit institutions lagged sadly behind that in the Netherlands and Britain. Even as late as at the time of Napoleon, the cautiousness of French banks led them to make only the most conventional (and well secured) of loans. Napoleon responded to the problem by conceiving of a great quasi-public bank which should receive government reserves on deposit as they accrued and should see that pending their disbursement they were used productively in (approved) private enterprises rather than being held as hoards in the private banks to which alternatively they might have been entrusted. The *Caisse des Dépôts et des Consignations* resulted in 1816. It was not merely a whim of Napoleon. It was a natural outgrowth of French conditions and attitudes.

The quality of private behavior and the tenor of government response which led to its establishment are echoed in further successive steps from 1816 to 1965. One of these steps was the development of the paternalistic relationship of the Bank of France to the commercial banks. To induce those banks to play the role in financing expanding business which the banks in Britain and the Netherlands played as a matter of course, there gradually developed in France a system by which the banks received assurance in advance of making a loan that the Bank of France would rediscount or purchase on request. With this advance assurance the banks dared to function. But they received no blanket guarantee. The condition of the assurance was in effect to give over to institutions intermediary between them and the Bank of France final judgment concerning specific types of loans and even specific loans. Only then would those institutions provide the endorsements needed for rediscounting. The disease fed on the remedy: because the Bank of France came close to underwriting loans, the peasant-like caution of the commercial banks could continue. And so the replacement of their judgment by that of quasi-governmental institutions continued. The formation of the *Crédit National* after World War I to be such an intermediary was not an innovation: it merely provided a convenient agency to continue an old and familiar function.

In these circumstances of private bank timidity, from time to time the French government also created its own specialized-investment institutions to finance activities deemed in the public interest from which private banks might shy away. Examples were loans for local government public works, loans to agriculture, and the financing of shipping companies. These institutions had existed long before the *Fonds de Développement Économique et Social* was created after World War II. The *Fonds* merely brought the several specialized government investment institutions under common management.

Not only financial institutions had long been accustomed to depend on government nurturance and guidance. The same had been true, though in lesser degree, of other economic enterprises. The government expected, and was expected, from long before the time of Napoleon, to decide which private ventures merited its support. This tradition continued. One of its manifestations, which seemed entirely normal to Frenchmen, was control by the government of issues of shares and bonds to determine not only that they were not fraudulent but also that they did not serve purposes of which the government disapproved. Like the other institutions of control which are important in French economic planning, this practice was not created for the purpose. The planners merely used the institutions which previous French attitudes—French national character—had caused to exist.

France: The Managers

The French bureaucracy bridges the political and economic fields. Each parliamentary group rationalized its intransigence by regarding itself as concerned not with means but with ends and regarding its ends as too sacred to permit either compromise or subordination to other national goals.[2] Perhaps partly for the same reason, as well as because of the bureaucrats' love of petty power and distrust in their own independent judgment, a similar rigidity pervaded the government bureaucracy. This is a situation found not only in France, but in France there seemed to be some parallelism between the mentality of parliamentary groups and that of the

bureaucracy. But above and somewhat outside the inflexible bureaucracy, there appeared at times a "super-bureaucracy" of experts.
While parliaments quarreled and broke down, were born and died,
the experts filled the gap by assuming broad discretionary power,
though within certain limits. They did so not reluctantly, *faute de
mieux,* but as a natural part of the social tradition. They took such
a function for granted. They liked it. They thought of themselves
not as intellectuals advising on public policies, but as businesslike
administrators. They came from the same background as French
businessmen and held much the same viewpoints. The ablest of them
were marked out for top positions from the time of their graduation
from the Ecole Polytechnique (which Napoleon, who saw the need
for such men to counteract French bureacratic tendencies, founded)
or from one of the other "great schools." They looked upon a government career as one among several channels in which they could
exercise managerial talents over large affairs. That they should
supervise banking policies, or even that in government offices should
exercise better business judgment than businessmen, would seem
natural in France.

The visibility of these men in government has varied greatly
from time to time, but they seem always to have been present, if
not in the civil service then in the quasigovernmental financial agencies or in private enterprises of national importance ready to be
called into government. When circumstances required and permitted, they have been "honest brokers" (Crozier's term), bridging
the gap between bureaucracy and business enterprise. But they have
been more than this. They have been top policy makers with great
initiative.

Thus, when Jean Monnet in 1946 formulated his plan for urgent
government aid and initiative to speed the reequipment of six industries, his action was reminiscent not only of the program for
national reequipment of the late 1920's but of earlier governmental
action extending back to, say, Colbert. And when experts of the
Commissariat au Plan invited the businessmen they thought most
capable to join them in formulating public policy, largely ignored
labor unions since the decisions being made concerned managerial
affairs, included discrimination in favor of some industries relative
to others and in favor of the more innovational (and powerful)
firms, and finally made adherence to the plan a condition for easy
access to the normal facilities of the financial markets, this did not

arouse general indignation among businessmen, workers, or the public. It seemed reasonable and natural, and the instruments to induce compliance with the plans were at hand. Both the making of plans in this way and the gathering together of the various well-established strands of influence over private economic action to implement the plans are merely a moderate extension of previous practice.

Britain: Mutual Accommodation

On the other hand, the operation of the principle that conflicts of interest should be settled by the attempt of reasonable men to understand each other's attitudes and reach an accommodation has been an outstanding factor in British history. Through several centuries while autocratic elite groups ruled in continental countries by the weight of tradition and if necessary by force, representative government broadened in Britain through the willingness of social groups to accommodate their conflicting viewpoints. In the process of seeking accommodation, power was exerted, but only once was it exerted to the ultimate. On all other occasions it seemed more decent to reach an accommodation. The exception occurred when Charles I, a king with alien traditions, sought to preserve his royal and religious power by force. The Civil War ensued, but when Charles I had been overthrown and executed, authoritarianism could not flourish in the British soil, even when rooted in intense religious feeling. It seemed wrong even to Cromwell himself, and it withered and died.

One of the most basic of British attitudes, then, has been that society is best served if differences among groups are settled by a process of mutual accommodation in which of course each will use the power at its disposal, but in a muted fashion. Jostling among individuals is distasteful to Britons; only in highly impersonal situations such as automobile driving does aggressiveness get rather free play. Similarly, jostling among groups is not entirely proper.[3] The relationships between the government and the public are comprehended within the principle: the power of government should be exerted only with restraint. The government should intervene to preserve public order or safety or to prevent the abuse of their power by strong private groups who do not sufficiently respect the virtue of self-restraint. Beyond the use of its power for these purposes, the government should intervene in the affairs of individuals or private groups only with the greatest of circumspection. And certainly it should discriminate among them only for the most compelling of reasons.

Britain: Rules to Govern Discretion

The principle that the government should intervene to prevent the abuse of their power by strong groups is so general that its pursuit could require the exercise of wide discretionary power by the government. But discretionary governmental power may be abused and must be both watched and limited. (Perhaps in no other country does the press devote so much attention to minor charges of the abuse of authority by a policeman or a local official. A British police officer does not order a suspected individual to come to the police station for questioning; he avoids the imputation of guilt by requesting the individual to come to the station because "we think you may be able to help us with our inquiries." The force of the "request" is the same in both cases.) To limit discretion, Britain has developed two criteria which, where they are pertinent, define the extent to which the government may intervene and the way it may intervene. One of these criteria is that the individual, as consumer, should be protected by the government against the insecurities created by industrialization. Even this principle was rather tardily adopted. Britain, the first industrial nation, followed France, Germany, and Sweden in the formulation of governmental measures for social welfare. The cost bore heavily on business firms, but only in accordance with general clearly defined criteria.

The other, which limits the discretion of the government at the same time that it serves to avert the tension of direct clashes among individuals, is the principle that in case of conflict of interests priority rests with the right of the individual not to be ejected from the position in which he has legally established himself. That is, the ethical rule is that in case of inability to reach a mutual accommodation, there is a *prima facie* judgment against the individual who seeks to disturb the prior situation.

The rule applies in individual as well as governmental action. It is, for example, the rule underlying the respect extended in Britain toward an individual's position in a queue. It probably enters into the intensity of opposition by many intellectuals in Britain to encroachment by the automobile upon existing patterns of living—the attitude that the desire of new automobile owners rushing about in pursuit of their pleasures does not justify disturbance of other persons who wish to preserve the prior situation. It may be a partial explanation of the degree of resistance of British industrial workers to technical change, which seems to be greater than on the Continent. In the public's attitudes toward government, this rule is no doubt an element in the approval of laws which protect any tenant's possession of living quarters with minimal adjustment of the level of rents he paid twenty-five years ago, in spite of the anomalies created by the intervening period of inflation and great population shifts.

Britain: A Man's Association Is His Castle

These two criteria, of course, cover only a small part of the area in which questions of the government's relationship to private power may arise. The dilemma created by the perception of a need to intervene combined with reluctance to intervene in the absence of clear nondiscretionary criteria, has been solved by the development of a relationship between government and private enterprise which is unique among modern nations. To a degree not known elsewhere, the principle governing domestic economic policy has been that if the problems of an industry or its power to affect the public welfare is so great that government intervention seems necessary, then the industry shall be taken into public ownership, so that the government is managing its own agent rather than intervening in private action; and that except where this seems necessary, private enterprises shall be left free of governmental regulation in which the element of regulatory discretion is strong.

Consider first the area of governmental ownership. As in most countries outside the United States of America, ownership by the central government or local government units of the group of industries broadly defined as public untilities came first. The railways remained an exception until after World War II. During the war, the government imposed centralized control even though the railways remained in private ownership. In peacetime this seemed improper and the government met railway problems, not by subsidy plus regulation of merger, closure, discontinuance of service, and so on, but by nationalization. Nationalization followed for three other industries whose common quality was that they had important impacts on the public welfare: road haulage because it is tinged with a public utility status and competes with the railways, coal mines because of the human impact of their economic problems, and steel because of its industrial importance. Because of the degree of intervention necessary in any event, almost no one in Britain would now propose that the problems within the coal and railway industries should be handled in any way but through government operations. The acts of nationalization had been by a Labour government. When the Conservative party came to power, it returned road haulage and steel to private hands. The eggs in the steel industry having been partially scrambled, the governmental Iron and Steel Board continued to exercise certain supervisory functions which to a limited degree violated the principle of nonintervention, but the road haulage industry, having been returned to private ownership with the exception of one company, was left less regulated than it is even in such a relatively *laissez faire* country as the United States.

Outside the sphere in which government seems necessary, the British government leaves business enterprise in general freer of regulation and intervention than probably any other industrial country except Japan [4]—or at least did so until 1965. The United States government is commonly regarded as much more *laissez faire* in its attitudes toward business than the British. But the senior author of this essay remembers vividly the amazement with which a British business executive who spent twelve months in the United States recently in contact with his American counterparts learned of the governmental regulations to which they had to tailor their actions and the relief and pleasure with which he described the relative freedom of British managers.

In particular, the British government has interfered less with the formation by individuals of firms of spontaneous associations to further their interests, and with their operations, than has probably any other government, again with the exception of Japan.[5] Giving sanction and unregulated freedom to spontaneous associations serves both the injunction against the undue use of government power and the principle that the resolution of differences by mutual accommodation is beneficial. When the tradition of the virtue of spontaneous association arose, the groups involved were mainly small ones whose action did not interfere too greatly with Adam Smithian "atomistic" competition. As circumstances changed and the associations became larger, more closely interrelated, and more powerful, the tradition continued. To a person from another country, associations of industrial employers on the one hand and trade unions on the other seem to be regarded in Britain as almost coequal in authority with the government, as embodying the public welfare rather than to be regulated in accordance with it, and as entities to be negotiated with rather than regulated. This is an exaggerated viewpoint, but it illustrates the difference in attitudes.

Trade unions are of course regarded in most industrial countries with great political respect. Yet in many other countries, to a greater degree than in Britain, it is regarded as proper for the government to impose its countervailing power against that of the unions. The sanctity accorded in Britain to the right to strike even in violation of agreements; the reluctance of the government to push a wage issue in a nationalized industry to the point of strike; and the even greater reluctance of the government to intervene against a strike in a private industry even if the direct effects of the strike are contrary to the public interest—all of these contrast sharply with the readiness of the French government to incur a strike in a nationalized industry if this is incidental to execution of its incomes policy and its use of troops to operate public utilities if a strike occurs.

The British economy is sufficiently closely knit so that in many industries competition long since ceased to be atomistic. The tendency in some industries to cartelization increased in the 1920's and the 1930's as a defense against the impact of the depression upon profits. Yet only in 1964 was legislation enacted to curtail the right of producers to enter into agreements with their retail dealers which prevent price competition. Such agreements protect small retail dealers whose turnover is so small that in the absence of resale price maintenance they would be forced out of business by the competition of the larger shops. Resale price maintenance thus has the virtue of protecting individuals in an established position against encroachment on that position by new dealers as well as the virtue of being an agreement freely arrived at among private groups. And only in 1965 has the legislation to deal with monopolistic agreements among business firms been amended to make it fully effective. Nor has the government regulated or supervised the business associations.

It is also reasonable to regard the concept that it is improper for the government to intervene in agreements reached by negotiation among spontaneous associations as at least a partial explanation of the failure of the government to take any action until 1964 and 1965 concerning severance pay and worker training.

Because of these uniquely British attitudes toward the role and status of private associations, it was almost inevitable that when the British government approached employers' and trade union associations with proposals for the establishment of economic planning machinery, it would do so, not as a representative of the public interest seeking the recommendations of groups with special interests before it exercised its authority, but as one association approaching two other associations to ask them what they would be willing to do.

During the period of negotiations French planning was held up as a model in many British discussions. However, French planning as visualized in the discussions was a process by which the government and the two sides of industry, meeting as equals, arrived at a target for future output and a sketch of a path to the target. This target and sketch, serving as an indication of what was possible, motivated the spontaneous efforts of individuals and firms.

As the discussion of Chapter VIII has indicated, this is a caricature of the French planning process. Its prevalence in the face of readily available facts is best explained, it would seem, by the assumption of the British groups concerned that this is the form to be expected in discussions between the government and private groups.

In any event, it was entirely in the nature of British institutions that the government approached the T.U.C. leaders and the leaders of the employers' organizations with no inducements in its pocket except the presentation of the principle that reasonable men should discuss their common problems, and that out of such a discussion— hardly a bargain, since the government had no counters with which to bargain—N.E.D.C. was born.

LABOUR'S NEW INSTITUTIONS: UNPRECEDENTED INTERFERENCE AND DISCRIMINATION

How, then, are the rather profound changes made or proposed by the Labour government to be explained? A summary of these changes, beginning with the least unprecedented measures, will emphasize their far-reaching nature. In its planning of education, of the country's transportation system, of land use, and of regional development, the Labour government is looking farther into the future than has been done in governmental planning at any time in the recent past. The government has altered the structure of the labor market by legislating new principles of dismissal compensation and by establishing worker training in many industries which apparently were not much interested in it. It has obtained for the Board of Trade the first really effective power to attack monopolies (except for the Conservative government's action in the one field of sale price maintenance). It has obtained advance notification to the government of wage claims or proposed price increases, and has announced its intention to obtain power to make any decision of the National Board for Prices and Incomes legally binding. In buying goods and services from firms, it will discriminate among them not on the basis of the prices quoted but on the basis of their steps to improve their efficiency. Perhaps most far-reaching of all, it has established a group of industrial advisers for the avowed purpose of influencing the managerial decisions of private firms.

The policy of altering the industrial framework and also intervening directly is entirely self-conscious. Discussing economic problems in February, the Prime Minister said: "We shall shortly be discussing with both sides of industry our plan for economic advance, a plan based on priorities, on priorities for those industries which can make the biggest contribution to exports, for the development of scientific and productive techniques, . . . a plan to strengthen our industrial base. . . . And this is going to mean tough and unpopular decisions in some cases. But it must be the Government, after seriously weighing all the advice that may be tendered to us, which takes these decisions and bears responsibility for them in Parliament and in the country." (*Sunday Times,* February 21, 1965.)

In part, the new directions in government policy are to be explained simply as results of traditional differences between the two parties. The two major parties have both accepted all of the values discussed above, but with different relative emphasis. The Labour party has always given much more weight to the need for the government to intervene against private power, and the Conservative party much more weight to the sanctity of spontaneous private association. The relevant differences in programs do not directly reflect class differences; they reflect differences in philosophy concerning the role of the government. If the actions which the Labour government is now taking are successful, they will disturb the lives of the persons who have traditionally been its constituents as much as they will those of other groups, for the winds of technical change blow sharply on some of the workers directly affected, even though they are kind to the working class as a whole. In the past the Labour party has advocated government intervention in economic affairs for the same purpose endorsed by the nation as a whole, purposes which may broadly be termed defensive ones. But because they favored more active intervention for these purposes, it was a smaller step for them than it would have been for the Conservatives to use that intervention in a discriminatory way to accelerate advance in productivity.

The concept of the machinery for planning which the Labour government has now established did not spring full blown from the minds of Harold Wilson or George Brown or from those of a group of 1964 Labour party leaders. The machinery bears a striking resemblance to that developed by the immediate postwar Labour government of which Harold Wilson was a member. In 1947 a Ministry of Economic Affairs was created. Sir Stafford Cripps was named Minister, and Harold Wilson was appointed to Sir Stafford's former post as President of the Board of Trade. Sir Stafford created a Central Economic Planning Staff, with an industrialist (now Lord Plowden) at its head. He created three agencies for consultation with industry: the Economic Planning Board, on which a small select group of industrialists met with senior civil servants; the National Production Advisory Council for Industry, for the discussion of production questions; and the National Joint Advisory Council, for the discussion of employer-employee relations. These are not closely paralleled by the National Economic Development Board which the Labour government inherited from its predecessor. But Sir Stafford also established Development Councils for various industries, which in several ways foreshadow the "little Neddies" as these have been reshaped by the present Labour government. To suggest that the present organization is due to lessons Mr. Wilson or his colleagues learned from Sir Stafford Cripps would be superficial, although it may be quite true of some specific bits of the machinery. The machinery established both times reflects a stream of thinking within the Labour party.

However, this is not the sole explanation. There are other influences at work. The Conservative government was also moving toward intervention. It was the Conservative government which enacted the law making resale price maintenance illegal (except under certain conditions). The action, it is true, was a great shock to some Conservative back-benchers, but they were too few to block it. It was also the Conservative government which used its economic power as a purchaser of the services of the construction industry to enforce moderate improvement in the methods of that industry. And the law that permits the government to levy on each of various industries a tax of some weight to finance a government-sponsored scheme of worker training in that industry was an inter-party measure, which could not have been taken without the initiative of the Conservative government, then in power.

There are some indications that the younger leaders of the Conservative party who advocated these measures, if given freedom to use their best judgment, would move in the general direction in which the Labour leaders have moved. On the other hand, some of the actions of the present Labour government are rather startling violations of the principles advocated by the older leaders of the Labour party and the trade union movement. There is therefore some reason to suggest both that change is occurring in both parties and that the emerging shape of planning is a response to the problems faced by the whole country. Perhaps it is also a resultant of intergenerational change in the values of the men facing these problems—a change, if you please, in "national character."

The men now possessing governmental authority in Britain give the impression of deciding without dogmatic preconceptions on measures to attack the problems facing them. It is as if they had said to themselves: "Given the national attitudes and the present national temper of Britain, what measures will induce changes in economic performance that will best meet the problems facing the country?" Having posed the question, they seem to select and institute measures with careful regard to their feasibility but without a second's thought concerning whether the measures violate former Labour party doctrines or, indeed, formerly accepted conventions concerning the economic role of government. They are not free agents. Of course they weigh the attitudes of Labour party members, of economic groups, and of the voters generally. They give the impression of doing so, with detachment, simply because they know they cannot continue to govern effectively unless they give heed to the beliefs and attitudes of the people on whose behalf they are governing.

This is not Machiavellian behavior. Decision without dogma is quite the opposite of decision without principle. Rather, this is behavior in the best tradition of service to the nation.

This does not imply that all of the decisions taken are the optimum ones. The judgments may be in error. Moreover, a case can be stated that, for the sake of the immediate emergency, measures are being taken that will result eventually in increased rigidities. The case can be stated, but it is difficult to conceive of considerations which should have priority over the lasting solution of the present emergency.

XI

Will Planning Succeed?

How great are the prospects that the government will succeed in its attempt to check inflationary pressures, accelerate the rate of increase in productivity, and preserve Britain's international financial position? Let us consider these three aspects of the economic problem in turn. It would be foolish to make flat predictions, but it is reasonable to evaluate the factors which will determine success or failure.

The analysis will assume that the Labour government remains in office. If it does not, the comments made below will require qualification. Yet the difficulties analyzed below will face any government and the discussion will be pertinent, *mutatis mutandis,* to the efforts of a Conservative government to resolve the same problems.

INFLATION

The government's incomes policy will succeed only with the sanction of the country's employers and union members. The machinery that has been created is as conductive to the attainment of assent to a noninflationary incomes policy as any which might be brought into existence in peacetime Britain. If what might be termed a "workable degree of consensus" is not reached, it will not be appropriate to lay the failure at the several doors of the planning machinery.

Yet a sanguine view of the likely success of the incomes policy hardly seems justified. Year after year since the end of the war, the

129

trade unions have pressed for wage increases greater than the economy's increase in productivity, that is, for an enlarged share of the national income. Year after year employers have acceded to the trade union pressure. Then they have raised prices to recoup the loss in profits they would otherwise suffer. The price rises in turn are part of the justification advanced by the unions for the next year's demands.

An attempt to explain the demands by unions as the result of the workers' belief that their living standards are not as good as they should be leads to bewilderment. For each year British workers are living better than they ever have before. Since there is no absolute standard of how high a level of living is merited, one that is increasing steadily would seem to be a satisfying one. If the contentment or discontent of workers were determined primarily by their level of material welfare, then each year, as they obtain increases of, say, 2½ per cent in real incomes, they might be expected to feel that life and the economic system are good.

Yet they are not content. Their unions press annually for wage increases of 4 or 5 or 6 or 10 per cent rather than for the increase which could be contained within the advance in productivity. It is crystal clear that they do so not because leaders advise the workers extravagantly, but because the workers themselves bear a perpetual feeling that life is not giving them all that it should.

In the view of one school of observers, this sense of "alienation" does not arise from the objective circumstances of the workplace. Rather it is a somewhat angry, somewhat anxious attitude, unverbalized, even unconscious, that is bred in the bones, so to speak, by the insecurity, anonymity, and rootlessness of industrial life. It seems to appear, sooner or later, in all industrial societies. The underlying anxiety and anger give rise to a pervasive hostility toward employers and a jealous fear by each group of workers that some other group may get a better deal.

In this view, annual demands for large wage increases are not merely means of getting more income. They are also ways of gaining emotional security from the strength of the union, satisfaction from the economic attack on the employers, and relief from the protection given against falling behind other groups of workers.

Unions give this reassurance, it is suggested, only if they are winning victories, not merely obtaining gains. To satisfy the need for successful attacks on employers, unions must extort from employers more than employers feel able to give. If by some miracle all of the increases in real income demanded in one year could be granted, workers would not then be content in subsequent years with wage increases within the limits of increases in productivity. Another attack would be necessary in the second year, and the third, and the fourth. For the sense of wrongness can never be lastingly relieved, but only temporarily appeased.

It should not be supposed that these attitudes are associated with a "public be damned" willingness to cause inflation. Rather they are associated with an assumption taken as axiomatic that employers, if they were not unwilling to dip into their bloated profits, could give all that is asked, and more. One of the striking characteristics of the comments of local British union leaders interviewed on television in 1965 concerning the government's incomes policy was the absence of any conception of a necessary relationship between 5 or 6 per cent annual increases in wages and inflation. That sincere and intelligent men are blocked by their perception of the nature of the world from considering that relationship illustrates the complexity of the problem. And, of course, the facts of limitations on competition in some areas of British industry provide an emotional basis for the perception.

The problem is accentuated in Great Britain by social attitudes that have dictated maintenance of a very high level of employment. Where it is politically necessary to maintain hyper-full employment, the dice are loaded in favor of continuing inflation. To achieve price stability in Britain it may be necessary to tolerate a level of unemployment of 2 per cent. However, the tightness of the labor market is only one of the forces which restrain employer resistance to wage increases beyond the limits of the national rate of increase in productivity. It is also true that it is no longer as virtuous as it once was to insist on the prerogatives of management and resist union demands. The same old phrases are uttered over lunch at the club, but today they have the ring of protesting too much. Employers feel a little guilty about behavior which once made them feel righteous—or which they once took for granted.

This view of the nature of the forces making for "cost-push" inflation need not be accepted without question, but it almost certainly contains important elements of truth. Nevertheless, the operation of these psychological forces is certainly influenced by economic, social, and political conditions. It is difficult to know what impact the present political situation in Britain will have. If industrial workers are told that in the national interest they must moderate their demands and that this will be without real cost to themselves, and if this advice comes from a sort of court established by a government in which they place a fair degree of trust, one has no reason to be sure that they will moderate their demands in consequence. For if the workers' sense of alienation exercises a pervasive influence on their thinking, then the advice to temper their demands will merely cause them to feel that even Labour party leaders are betraying them. To counter this betrayal they may seek the more bitterly to win their contest with their employer each year. Even trade union leaders who counsel moderation and cooperation with an incomes policy may thereby be sacrificing their own following rather than influencing their unions.

An attitude that might be more influential would be a sense of participating in a great national effort. If this sense of their contribution to the nation complemented union membership as a source of emotional security, cooperation in a national effort might soften worker demands for union aggressiveness. Or, if such a sense of participation touched most industrial workers, the pressure of their censure might restrain somewhat the unions that are traditionally the most aggressive. However, some sense of unity between workers and employers would be required, and an observer who predicted this effect would be rash indeed. A national leader would be equally rash if he attempted deliberately to inculcate that attitude, for exhortation to workers, or striking a pose, might instead deepen the impression in the minds of workers that they were being used.

PRODUCTIVITY

Pessimism about price stability need not be accompanied by pessimism about accelerating the pace of advance in productivity. The two depend on different factors: advance in productivity is within the control of managers to a much greater degree than is price stability.

Worker Attitudes

It is true that deep-seated attitudes of workers (not merely union restrictions) are also a part of this problem. Somehow, out of the class frictions of British society and the deep unemployment of the 1920's and 1930's there has developed strong labor resistance to pressure from management and to technical change. As far as can be judged from the available unsystematic comparisons, this resistance in Britain has been more rigid during the postwar period than that seen in other countries of Western Europe or the United States. The British workers' attitude that foremen shall "keep off their backs" rather than check too closely on their use of their time seems more rigid than that in the other countries mentioned. Small craft groups in Britain often cling to their traditional tasks and stubbornly resist technical change, and in the name of worker solidarity their mates support the practice. Much continental practice, on the other hand, invites the assignment of workers to tasks outside their own craft, on the ground that diversified experience increases job security. Even if it is incorrect that these attitudes inimical to change are stronger in Britain than in other Western countries, clearly they are present and make increase in productivity more difficult.

Some of these attitudes arise out of the workers' earlier life experience, including childhood, and may not be greatly affected by the work environment. However, many of them are also affected by the work atmosphere. Managers who are sufficiently insightful and capable to meet worker needs for security and recognition find introducing new techniques easier.

The authors of a well-known study of a group of British coal mines found that of the work performed on each shift, on the average one-third consisted of duplication of preparatory work done by the previous shift, or of otherwise wasted time. However, the authors also concluded that this situation was largely a result of the nature of work organization in these mines which had come about as a by-product of the introduction of new machines, and might be remedied in large part if that organization were changed.[1] In 1960 the Esso Petroleum Company signed an agreement with the various craft unions to which its workers belonged, providing for widespread abandonment of jurisdictional restrictions on each worker's tasks in return for sizable wage increases and guarantees of job security—guarantees the company was able to give because of its plans for expansion of production. In 1965 the Mobil Oil Company negotiated an even more comprehensive agreement with its unions. These agreements indicate that elimination of restrictive practices by competing unions may be achieved if sufficient financial inducements are possible, if job security is not threatened, and if there is mutual confidence between the employer and the unions.

Managerial Behavior

Many British observers are pessimistic about the attitudes of British managers toward administrating technical innovation. Some of their comments are cited here, not as clear evidence concerning the facts, but as evidence of the national temper of self-criticism.

A leading British sociologist has calculated, from surveys in Britain and the United States, that the work week of British managers is about one-fourth shorter than that of their American counterparts.[2] The samples were too small to attach great weight to the precise fraction, but the author of the article believes that a significant difference clearly exists.

Another recent observer noted that many of the more effectively innovational senior managers in British industry are ethnically or culturally not British. Many were born abroad, a number in Canada, some are Jewish; the designer of the strikingly successful Mini Minor automobile is Greek.[3]

The writer of a leading article in the *Economist* for December 26, 1964, entitled "Britons Will Be Slaves," suggested two basic causes of "Britain's disappointing economic performance" since World War II:

> First, too many British people in their workaday lives instinctively hate anything modern or new, while it is nowadays more common for the most efficient foreigners to be instinctively captivated by it. . . . Secondly, the British . . . will go to extraordinary lengths to shun uncongenial and (especially) embarrassing tasks—even when the dictates of efficiency and profitability make it quite obvious that these are the tasks that most need to be tackled.

The problem is not one that attracts top management only, and comment on it is not new. . . . In talking of the low standard of discipline, endeavour, and innovation in British management, during his inaugural lecture at Sheffield University this month, the new Professor of Applied Economics there said sagely that he believed this attitude to business was "an integral part of many of the cultural patterns which we find most attractive in British society, its relative freedom from tensions and anxiety, its easy-going good nature, its uncompetitiveness."

Lest the reader think that there may be some political or social bias in these comments, it may be noted, lastly, that the director of the Conservative Political Research Centre (writing in a personal capacity) suggested in a 1965 pamphlet that among many British firms there is "nagging doubt whether higher productivity and greater efficiency are the kind of goals after which decent people should be chasing." [4]

It is worthwhile to repeat that the tone of self-criticism in these comments is not merely or necessarily an objective recognition of facts; it itself is a part of the national temper, worthy of separate note. A contrast with the American society will illustrate the point. The rate of increase in output per worker in the United States during the past decade has hardly been more than ¼ per cent per year faster than that in Britain.[5] Yet industrial managers in the United States regard themselves as vigorous, effective, and innovational, and American observers also regard them thus; whereas not only British observers such as these quoted here but also British managers, except in the few leading firms, seem continually on the defensive.

It is entirely possible that the present British temper is a prelude, not to an admission of defeat, but to an increase in the effectiveness of management. It is not an unknown sociological phenomenon that individuals are goaded to new and more effective action if peers whom they have regarded as no more effective, or perhaps less effective, than themselves begin to surpass them. There has long been belief in Britain of the superior ruthlessness and effectiveness of American managers, but these have seemed a special faraway group, operating in a crass environment, whose behavior one neither could nor would desire to emulate. There has been somewhat the same view of the Germans. However, when not only the Germans but also the French and even the Italians began to outperform them, the comparison perhaps caused a different reaction. And when a conspicuous number of the most effective managers within Britain are culturally immigrants, the uneasiness may be the greater.

There are some bits of positive evidence that a rather profound change of temper is occurring. Among them is the fact that a handful of oustanding industrial and business managers have left their firms for a period of two years or more to work under a Labour government to accelerate Britain's rate of increase in productivity or curb the price spiral. The most conspicuous of these moves are that of Mr. H. F. R. Catherwood from the managing directorship of British Aluminium, Ltd., to become chief industrial adviser in the Department of Economic Affairs and that of Mr. Duncan Dewdney from the corresponding position in the Esso Petroleum Company to be deputy director of the Board for Prices and Incomes. His acceptance of this thankless position is even more remarkable than that by Mr. Catherwood and his colleagues of positions as industrial advisers. Surely none of these men will advance his industrial career by this diversion from his industrial position. That these men have accepted these positions, and that their companies have been willing to release them while holding their positions open, is impressive testimony to the sense of a social purpose and a duty to serve it which must motivate both the individuals and their companies. Perhaps it is evidence of a wider current, promising heightened achievement by British managers as a group.

The attitudes of labor may be changing also. The Esso and Mobil productivity agreements are only the most spectacular examples of a larger number which have been reached. Still others seem to be in the wind. It is possible that in an economy of full employment the resistance of workers toward work changes is softening, or that the factors—whatever they are—which have influenced the temper of management have been influencing workers as well.

THE CONTRIBUTION OF PLANNING

There is, therefore, at least some basis for speculating that a fairly fundamental social change is occurring. If so, Britain's economic performance throughout the next decade may markedly surpass that during the last. This is not a forecast, but only the statement of a possibility. If the change should occur, governmentally guided planning will probably be among the lesser of the causes. However, the possible contribution of planning should be noted.

Indicative Planning

To some persons, "planning" consists primarily in the preparation of a "plan" for a certain number of years which estimates the possible increases in productivity in various industries, and on the basis of these increases in productivity plus the expected increase in the labor force presents targets for output for sectors of the economy and the nation as a whole and estimates the amount of investment needed to create the required productive capacity. Because such a projection would also indicate the size of future markets thought to be available for various industries, expansion of productive capacity to that indicated in the plan is assumed to occur.

Undoubtedly, such a plan does have considerable importance. However, the nature of the conviction carried by a government plan should not be misunderstood. The larger companies certainly prepare their own estimates of future markets, and they will not regard an outside estimate as more reliable than their own simply because it was prepared by a government department. Indeed, large and small companies alike are conscious that they, not the government, will suffer financial loss if they create too much capacity and may regard the government estimate as less responsible than their own. Nevertheless, if enough technical information is available to the governmental planners and if it is capably used, the plan will indicate the probable interindustry relationships at a future level of production—the market for each industry's products provided by their use as components in the production of other industries—more effectively than a projection of future demand by any one company or industry is likely to do. The plan may thus indicate markets whose size a given industry had underestimated. If the projections of total output and interindustry relationships are convincingly presented, these indications may be persuasive and may convince some industries to construct a greater increase in capacity than they otherwise would.

Examples of the possible effects of a plan, and the limitations of them, are provided by forecasting errors in recent years in the chemical, machine tool, and cement industries. For the first two there have been steadily increasing imports, and in the last a burst of imports which attracted much attention in the early months of 1960. In the machine tool industry, judging by discussions in the press, many foreign machine tool makers have been able to sell in Britain because they have advanced beyond British producers in design. They have done this not merely because of their greater ingenuity but because British tool makers have been more timid than some others about committing themselves to the overhead costs required for the production of specialized machines when the size of the market was uncertain. On the other hand, British firms can and do produce many of the chemicals whose imports have been growing. But they have produced them in inadequate amounts because in a fluctuating market producers either underestimated the rise in demand or preferred the risk of inadequate capacity to that of excess capacity. In the event, some decisions in both industries seem to have been cautious in a degree that was unprofitable to the industry and costly to the country. The market forecasts involved are ones affected by a variety of special influences, some of which an overall plan would provide no help in judging. Yet a well-integrated projection concerning future markets might lead to some improvement in even such specialized forecasts.

The cement industry presents a contrasting case. It is typical of the many for which a well-integrated projection of future production would much more certainly lead to an improvement in forecasting. While some types of construction use much more cement than others, these tend to average out so that the aggregate market for cement largely depends simply on the total volume of construction in the country, plus changes in that volume which lead to changes in the cement stocks needed by dealers and builders to service the changed flow of activity. From 1963 to 1964 the volume of construction activity rose by the remarkably large ratio of 12 per cent and the demand for cement, according to the Cement Makers' Federation, rose by 22 per cent. Because of the crippling winter of 1962–63, demand in 1963 was somewhat below its longer-term trend; hence a larger than usual rise from 1963 to 1964 should have been expected. One of 22 per cent could hardly have been anticipated, but in a competitive industry of growing demand a fair margin of precautionary excess capacity would normally exist. However, because of limitations in productive capacity in the cement industry, production of cement could be increased in 1964 by only some 18 per cent, not enough to meet the demand, and makers were forced to import cement.

One may reasonably ask whether their earlier planning of productive capacity had been appropriately geared to the absolutely certain longer-term upward trend in construction. The question is the more pertinent in view of the industry's attitude in mid-1965. At this time, when the backlog of the country's construction needs indicated a volume of construction activity steadily rising through an indefinitely long future period, the chairman of the country's largest cement producing company announced the expectation that demand would "return to normal." (*Guardian,* June 29, 1965.) Demand may of course fall temporarily, since that in 1964 reflected in part an unusually large increase in stocks. But if the comment implies the attitude that the normal level of demand is a constant, then a "plan" may induce an important correction in the industry's foresight. A similar effect may be induced, gradually if not quickly, in some other industries.

Positive Planning

A national plan may thus improve the planning of future capacity and production by individual industries and companies. Even if it does, and if the corrections increase company estimates of future demand and thereby induce increased investment, it should not be assumed that they will necessarily step up advance in productivity greatly. As has been suggested in Chapter IV, the notions that technical advance is stimulated primarily by expectation of an increased market and that an expansion of capacity necessarily increases output per worker are fallacious. Production on an increased scale does in some cases permit the use of more efficient methods and in some cases an accelerated increase in productivity will occur. But even if it does not, increased expansion due to a better view of the future market will reduce future dependence on imports. If only that result occurs, and even in only a few cases, the preparation of the plan will be handsomely justified.

Preparation of the plan may be influential on the government itself. For the government carries out many of the economic activities which need to be planned with the longest look to the future. The exercise of looking some years ahead, and then pondering the implications of that projection if carried still farther into the future, may stimulate a more imaginative examination of future transport, communication, worker training, and general education needs than would otherwise occur and may also stimulate more vigorous efforts to overcome resistance to change. Power needs, of course, also must be anticipated some years in advance. However, the planning of future power needs is in some ways much simpler than planning for the other needs, and power planning may perhaps be as adequate without as with the integrated sketch of the future provided by a plan. After costly power deficiencies in Britain in the early 1960's, and a very tight power position even for 1966, because of incompetent planning in the 1950's, power planning now seems adequately bold and vigorous to do without the guidelines provided by the plan.

The plan for 1970 will be of special importance in planning foreign trade policies. This prospect is discussed in the concluding section of this chapter.

Nevertheless, in the writer's view the formulation of a plan is a less important component of planning than are various other measures designed directly to stimulate increase in productivity. Planning defined in the broadest sense includes all such measures. Let us consider them briefly.

It is conventional to begin with the creation of an environment favorable to business enterprise. Here many critics give the Labour government poor marks; they suggest that various provisions of the tax on company profits being enacted by the 1965 Parliament will deter risk-taking and innovation. Even on conventional lines of argument, one may be skeptical that this is correct. When one tots up the incentives and disincentives in the new legislation, it comes out fairly well. But it is more important to note that financial incentives are by no means the only motor of modern capitalism. Improvement in the financial environment is not the explanation of the great postwar acceleration in innovation in France, Germany, and Italy relative to any previous period, or that in Yugoslavia, or that in Japan. Rather, using a loose phrase as a catch-all for a complex of factors not fully understood, one may say that a new spirit of enterprise is at work. The change is, so to speak, within managers and workers, rather than merely in the environment around them. Perhaps it is not an overstatement that planning in Britain will succeed only in so far as it invigorates management and labor.

One may hope that the training of skilled manpower to be carried out under the Industrial Training Act of 1964 will improve the skills of industrial workers sufficiently to more than justify its cost; that the payroll levy for compensating workers who become superfluous and the alterations in unemployment compensation will help to make labor more mobile; and that enforcement of the anti-monopoly legislation of 1965 will somewhat decrease cartelization in the economy. These measures may turn out to be extremely useful. Nevertheless, they prove far less important than the direct intervention of the government via its role as purchaser, research contractor, and grantor of credit, and through the work of that new wine poured into bottles a few months old, the "new" "little Neddies."

Among hindrances to accelerated advance in productivity, the "little Neddies" may pinpoint: technical backwardness or restrictionism by labor or management; insufficiently imaginative investment policies which have resulted in bottlenecks when demand rose; ineffective arrangements for management training and development or for joint consultation with workers' representatives; inadequate market research; lack of feasible standardization; remediable circumstances in the economy outside the industry which impinge on the industry; and many others. (In *Thrusters and Sleepers,* a 1965 publication of Political and Economic Planning, four economists who did research on the subject note the superiority among the more innovational and profitable firms of management training and development, procedures for consultation with workers' representatives, use of management consultants and market research. In industries where there are numerous small firms with somewhat lethargic managements, the "little Neddies" may become aware of deficiencies the firms involved have not themselves recognized. They may suggest mergers which the small firms had not been imaginative enough to think of. In other industries, they may indicate solutions which were not clearly visualized by managers, or may strengthen the resolution of managers to take the somewhat painful steps necessary to carry out the remedies. Moreover, they may call the government's attention to problems lying, so to speak, in the interstices between industries.

The "little Neddies" *can* do these things. It does not necessarily follow that they will. Americans familiar with the ineffectiveness of, say, the federal Small Business Administration and its successors may tend to assume that they will not. The formation of "little Neddies," and proposals by them, are at best only preludes to the necessary action.

However, the precision with which the recently formed "little Neddies" have been focused on areas where action is both important and feasible is impressive. Impressive also are the managerial capabilities or technical knowledge, or both, of the industrial advisers and of the chairmen of a number of the "little Neddies." Moreover, the composition of the "little Neddies" gives reasonable assurance that they can, if they will, probe the problems of their industries. Some have already evinced a tendency toward a detached and constructively critical view of their industries. If the sense of a need for action motivates them more deeply than self-interest has motivated industrial managers, they may be highly effective.

The chairmen of "little Neddies" and the industrial advisers are men who are respected as individuals and for their business judgment and who will speak as friends from within industry, not as critics from without. They will come offering specific suggestions, not merely criticisms. They will come with the practical and sometimes the formal authority to offer inducements or indicate pressures from the government. Their analyses will be the more effective if, as the straws in the wind suggest may often be the case, they coincide with a sense of a need for change felt by industrialists themselves.

Indeed, the intervention will be effective only if it does coincide with such a sense of a need for change. For managerial changes must be made within firms; by definition, they cannot be instituted from without.

These measures to prod and to induce cannot be introduced and continued solely by the decision of a government, even one with a larger parliamentary majority than that of the 1965 Labour government. Unless there is willingness among a large part of the public to accept the pains of accelerated change, a government increasing those pains may be brought down by the defection of many of its supporters. But perhaps the present temper of Britain is such that that sanction will be given. Whether it will continue to be given will be affected by many seemingly unrelated matters, such as the repercussions on popular emotions of foreign policy decisions and the judgment of the nation whether actions of the government are in the main ones of principle or expediency. Assuming that it does continue to be given, the unconventional measures now being executed may be effective.

In a sense the new measures are radical ones. They imply that private industry not motivated to efficient performance by the traditional motives of capitalism may be galvanized by scrutiny from without administered in the name of the public interest. Government arousing capitalism from its lethargy? Few philosophies could be more radical than this. Yet, like the Rooseveltian New Deal in the United States, the Labour government's measures are also profoundly conservative, for their purpose is to reinforce capitalism, not to encroach upon it; to invigorate it, not to replace it. There is no implication, it may be repeated, that British capitalism has retrogressed in vigor, but only that it has not matched the unprecedented pace of achievement of Britain's neighbors. With the aid of governmental planning of this unprecedented nature, it may now do so. But perhaps, as I have suggested in Chapter VII, its vigor was increasing in any event.

The world is waiting to apply a harsh test of success, the trend in Britain's balance of payments.

THE BALANCE OF PAYMENTS: THE BATTLE OF 1964–65

The Labour government inherited a balance-of-payments crisis when it took office in mid-October, 1964. The nation's international payments had exceeded her earnings by threatening amounts throughout the first eight months of the year, and the Bank of England had been forced to sell gold repeatedly to meet the required payments in foreign currencies. Then, early in October, the Treasury's monthly report on the gold reserves indicated not only that a further decline in the country's holdings of gold and convertible currencies had occurred but also that additional withdrawals of funds had been met by an undisclosed amount of borrowing from the Federal Reserve Bank of New York, the Bank of Canada, and six European central banks. This meant that the withdrawal of funds had exceeded the decline in reserves by some amount which the government chose not to reveal. The September trade returns, released a few days later, showed a sharp drop in exports in September. The fear of eventual devaluation, heightened by these developments, may have been heightened further by the Labour party's victory in the election because of a suspicion that a Labour government would not be as willing to depress economic activity in the country to defend the pound as a Conservative government would have been.

The Magnitude of the Crisis

Out of this set of circumstances, when the Labour government was elected, a "run on the pound" threatened. Indeed, the September figures of currency withdrawals suggested that it might already have begun.

During the first three quarters of the year, Britain's payments to abroad had exceeded her receipts from abroad by an average of some 50 million pounds per month, and the deficit seemed to be increasing. The significance of this rate of drain is seen by comparing it with the total of Britain's reserves of gold and foreign currencies. The total withdrawal of funds from Britain during 1964 was 721 million pounds. Of this a small fraction, possibly no more than one-tenth, consisted of speculative withdrawals late in the year by depositors who feared for the future of the pound.[6] The remaining net withdrawals—probably about 650 million pounds of the total—were due to the excess of payments over receipts on normal transactions. This sum was greater than Britain's total holdings of gold plus foreign currencies at the end of the year, apart from those she had obtained by borrowing from foreign central banks and monetary institutions. If this rate of net outflow had continued, even without further speculative withdrawals Britain would have no monetary reserves whatever by the end of 1965 other than those she could borrow. In fact, because of speculative withdrawals Britain reached this position by the end of July, 1965. The British government also held some 450 million pounds of United States securities, which in the last resort could be sold to obtain funds.

The underlying situation was revealed in more detail in balance-of-payments data for 1964 (first released in May, 1965, and revised in September). These are presented in the table below. This table and the two paragraphs that follow it may be omitted by the reader without loss of continuity.

MONETARY MOVEMENT, 1964
(Millions of Pounds)

Long-term investment, net	—344
Exports and imports *	—534
"Invisibles," current account	+122
"Balancing item"	+35
Net monetary movement	—721

* Both valued f.o.b.

The net outflow of funds labeled long-term investment in this tabulation consisted of intergovernmental loans by the United Kingdom (minus repayments on previous loans), net withdrawals by foreign companies and individuals of funds invested in long-term securities or property in Britain, and net investment of funds abroad by British companies and individuals. This outflow plus payment for the unprecedented excess of imports over exports was offset in part by an inflow of funds on account of the so-called invisible current items. These consist of three main groups. First, payments and receipts for services performed (the earnings of the private sector of the economy on freight, insurance, tourism, and other private services) were moderately in excess of payments to abroad for similar services. These net earnings, however, were more than offset by governmental expenditures (predominantly the military) abroad, so that the balance of the two was an estimated outflow of about 75 million pounds. Second, Britain's net receipts of dividends and interest from investments abroad exceeded the corresponding payments to abroad by some 400 million pounds. Third, however, this large contribution to the balance of payments was partly offset by withdrawals by foreign governments, companies, and individuals of funds they had on deposit or invested in short term securities in Britain. The net withdrawals of such funds amounted to an estimated 208 million pounds.[7] Most of this was accounted for, not by an excess of speculative withdrawals over high-interest-seeking inflows, but rather by withdrawals by foreign countries, members of the sterling area, who had deficits in their own balances of payments and met them by drawing on their deposits in Britain. The net of these three sets of flows on account of "invisibles" was a recorded inflow of 122 million pounds.

As is the case every year, in addition to these recorded totals for long-term investment, trade, and current "invisibles," there was an added net inflow of funds (which may have been for any or all of these purposes) which somehow escaped the recording network. In 1964, though smaller than usual, this was some 35 million pounds. The total outflow of funds would have been even greater than 721 million pounds if capital and interest on United States loans, totaling somewhat more than 50 million pounds, had been paid on schedule. The United States government agreed to postponement of these payments.

Precise data concerning the balance of payments and the monetary reserves were not known publicly in October, 1964, because the balance-of-payments data can be compiled only some months after the fact, and because the state of the monetary reserves was not fully revealed. But the nature and general magnitude of the balance-of-payments problem was clear.

The Battle

The Labour government's first steps prevented any immediate crisis, but they did not end a steady outflow of gold. For approximately eleven months, while the outflow continued and it was not clear whether the drain might force Britain to devalue, foreign central banks and monetary institutions lent Britain funds to meet the outflow, and during this period the government of Britain took a series of measures to reduce outpayments, increase foreign exchange earnings, restore confidence, and bring the drain to an end.

The more important measures are outlined in the following paragraphs.

Immediately after the election, the new government acted to curtail imports, by imposing a 15 per cent surtax on industrial imports, and to stimulate exports, by granting exporters certain tax rebates—the only ones permitted under international agreements. These amounted to some 2 per cent of the total value of exports. Early in November, while announcing fulfillment of its promise to increase certain social benefit payments, the government also announced tax increases that more than matched them. On November 23 the Bank of England raised the Bank Rate—the rate at which it advances funds to commercial banks—from 5 to 7 per cent. It used to be said that this crisis rate, together with the tight credit policy it signals, would "draw money from the moon." (The rate was reduced to 6 per cent in June, 1965.)

At about the same time, the Chancellor of the Exchequer announced that the April 1965 budget would include changes in tax laws designed both to lessen the advantage of investing abroad relative to investing at home and to induce an increased remittance of profits to Britain from the foreign subsidiaries of British companies. Before budget time, the Minister of Defence announced cancellation of the development of a very expensive supersonic bomber in order both to reduce government expenditures and to free engineers and technicians for other work. When the Chancellor presented the budget in April, he announced the new tax laws, plus curtailment of some government spending plans. He announced also an increase from 20 to 25 per cent in the minimum down payment on consumer durable goods purchased. Early in May, the Bank of England "requested" (that is, ordered) commercial banks to limit to 5 per cent the increase in their loans during the year ending in March, 1966.

Throughout the early months of 1965 a series of measures to reduce the outflow or increase the inflow of funds was put into effect. The criteria for granting permission to buy foreign exchange for "direct" investment abroad—investment by British companies in companies abroad which they manage or will manage—were tightened. A variety of other administrative controls were tightened. For example, the regulations concerning tourists' purchases of foreign exchange had been rather easily evaded in the past by buy-

ing traveler's checks at several banks. A change in the regulations
made this impossible. The conditions under which an individual
might buy foreign exchange to purchase a house abroad were restricted. One-fourth of the proceeds of the sale of various "dollar"
assets was required to be sold to the Treasury, rather than being
held abroad by the sellers. And so on. The government also pledged
itself to reduce its own payments abroad, mainly the military ones,
for example by reducing the size of its armed forces in Germany if
it was not able to negotiate German purchases of British equipment
to offset them. In July the government announced that the West
German government had agreed to make military purchases from
Britain equal to the foreign exchange costs of maintaining the
British "Army of the Rhine," and had deposited 41 million pounds
in London as a fund against which the purchases would be charged.

Late in July the Chancellor announced the most drastic set of
measures yet: a six-month postponement of many government and
local authority capital expenditure programs, deferment of some
new social security measures, reduction of the maximum consumer
durable payment period from thirty-six to thirty months, controls
which would curtail private investment except in housing and factories, and further restrictions on the use of funds for investment
abroad.

The import surcharge had been reduced to 10 per cent at the
end of April to mollify the E.F.T.A. countries; the remaining 10
per cent surcharge was obviously going to be maintained for some
time. (In the autumn the Chancellor announced that it would
probably remain until at least the end of 1966.)

These measures—and the list above is not complete—were not
planned successive steps in a unified campaign. Rather, each additional measure was resorted to as it became evident that the previous ones had not checked the currency drain.

The actions late in 1964 had perhaps been somewhat ineptly
taken. The import surcharge had been imposed without prior consultation with Britain's E.F.T.A. partners. This lack of consultation
alarmed and angered them.[8] Their reaction suggested that it might
seem politically necessary to remove or reduce the levy before doing
so was justified economically. This effect may have provoked some
flight from sterling. Moreover, the failure to apply any fiscal or
monetary squeeze on the economy raised the old question whether

the Labour party leaders were willing to give up their social goals in order to defend the pound. A deflationary squeeze on the economy was regarded in some financial circles as the only true test of a government's determination. When, early in November, the Chancellor announced part of the social expenditure program promised before the election at the same time that he announced tax increases, this again created uncertainty.

Finally, the rise in the Bank Rate in November was not handled crisply. After an address by the Prime Minister on Wednesday, November 18, concerning the economic situation, the Bank Rate was not raised on Thursday, the usual day for such changes. It has been suggested that lack of action on that day was at the request of officials of the United States Federal Reserve system, who were reluctant to impose the rise in rediscount rates in the United States that would be necessary if the British Bank Rate rose. The Bank Rate was raised to 7 per cent on the following Monday, but the delay increased uncertainty concerning the British government's determination to defend the pound.

(As became known later, one important reason why no more drastic action was taken in October or November was the anticipation that a downturn in industrial activity was imminent in any event. The index of industrial production, which had ceased to rise early in 1964, remained constant throughout most of the year. A 1965 revision of the 1964 index showed that industrial production had in fact been rising throughout almost the entire year, but until that revision was made there was no reason to suppose that the index was in error.)

These suspicions concerning Labour attitudes, combined with knowledge that the trade deficit was not inordinately high, resulted in the commonly expressed judgment during the months that followed that much of the drain of funds late in 1964 and throughout the first months of 1965 would not have occurred except for distrust of the Labour government's firmness. In view of the underlying payments trends, summarized above, it is clear that this was incorrect. The relationship between normal payments and receipts was in itself sufficient to cause a continuing drain.

Month after month, the trade results fluctuated. The excess of imports over exports fell, then rose again. Perhaps there was an improving trend, but this was far from certain. During the first six months of 1965, exports were 4 per cent higher in value than a year earlier, but toward mid-year they seemed to be leveling off. Then in July they soared, and imports fell. But in August, exports fell, and imports rose. Month after month also, the demand by holders of sterling for foreign currencies continued. The demand was met partly by drawing on Britain's stock of gold and partly by drawing on successive loans from foreign central banks and the International Monetary Fund. Since month by month the Treasury announced only the net reduction in monetary reserves, without stating how much additional demand had been met by borrowing, no one could know just how grave the situation was.

However, in June many holders of sterling deposits seemed to reach a firm decision that Britain would lose. A surge of speculative withdrawal occurred during June through August; total withdrawals during those months were very large. In addition, throughout the spring and summer months, many depositors and business firms purchased from the Bank of England contracts for the delivery of foreign currency three months in the future. These forward purchases created obligations on the Bank of England which might put the monetary reserves in jeopardy when the contracts came due. (The purpose of such contracts is to insure that the foreign currency will be obtained at the exchange rate prevailing when the contract is made, rather than at the less favorable one which will be in effect if devaluation occurs before the currency is needed. Such contracts involve some cost to the buyers; they are made only if the buyer thinks insurance against the risk of devaluation—or fluctuation in the exchange rate—is worth the cost.)

When the Chancellor's July announcements indicated a willingness to use deflationary measures even though unemployment had already begun to increase, devaluation seemed somewhat less likely.

While the speculative withdrawals had caused a large drain of funds, they had also reduced the amount of funds held by foreigners who might withdraw them for speculative reasons. In August, it appeared that the Bank of England probably possessed enough gold and foreign currencies to meet all the additional short-term withdrawals that might possibly be made. True, all of these reserves had been borrowed, but they were nevertheless available. Then, early in September, the government administered a stroke which completely punctured the speculation against the pound. This was an arrangement for additional loans of unspecified amount from a group of central banks, an arrangement which made it appear likely that Britain would be able to meet additional demands for foreign currencies or gold for an indefinite period. The speculators caved in, money flowed back into Britain—61 million pounds in September and 42 million pounds in October, in addition to unspecified amounts used to repay debts to foreign central banks. For the time being at least, the short-term battle was won.

In addition to these measures, certain fortuitous events will aid Britain's balance of payments in the near future. The 60 million pound investment by Shell in the Italian company Montecatini will not be repeated (controls on direct investment abroad can see that it is not), and the drilling in the North Sea by foreign oil companies will result in 1965 in a sizable flow of expenditures in Britain. One should not stress such "accidental" changes too heavily, for the entire flow of payments and receipts consists of a shifting aggregate of miscellaneous items, many of them nonrecurrent but replaced by others; and such favorable shifts may always be offset by adverse ones. But perhaps these are net favorable changes apart from the usual flux of payments and receipts.

The Chancellor of the Exchequer has expressed the judgment that as the measures discussed above work their effects the excess of Britain's payments to abroad over her receipts from abroad will shrink sufficiently so that payments and receipts will be in balance by the end of 1966. Let us begin an analysis of the longer-term problem by considering what the state of Britain's reserves of gold and foreign currencies will be at the end of 1966 if the Chancellor's forecast is correct.

At the beginning of September, 1965, Britain's published reserves were 923 million pounds. Her indebtedness to foreign central banks and the International Monetary Fund was 1150 million pounds or slightly less.[9] She thus owed some 230 million pounds more than the reserves in her possession. Her payments of normal types to abroad were undoubtedly still running above her receipts. However, perhaps 400 million pounds of the withdrawals during the preceding year had been speculative—that is, motivated by fear of devaluation. It is reasonable to assume that before this essay is in print in the spring of 1966, these 400 million pounds will have been returned to London. They will make good the excess of indebtedness over reserves and leave a balance of 170 million pounds. If for convenience we assume that this is the amount of the deficit in normal receipts and payments during the last four months of 1965 and all of 1966, we may assume that Britain's reserves will be just equal to her indebtedness at the end of 1966.

This assumption may be in error by, say, 100 million pounds, but it will be sufficiently close to correct to provide a point of departure for discussion of the longer-term problem. Britain must both repay her debts and increase her monetary reserves. Her receipts from abroad must be made dependably greater than her payments to abroad. The central problem of her economic policy is whether this can be done.

THE BALANCE OF PAYMENTS: THE WAR OF 1966–70

An evaluation of whether it can be done may begin with brief further consideration of the causes of the 1964–65 crisis.

The Forces at Work

The cause commonly assigned is well known: Britain has become progressively less able to compete with other industrial nations in international markets. Her percentage share of the world's industrial exports fell from about 21 per cent to about 14 per cent between 1963 and 1964, and on the other hand her imports of industrial products were becoming an increasing percentage of her own industrial production. Between 1953 and 1964 the physical volume of exports rose by somewhat less than 3½ per cent per year, while the physical volume of imports rose by 4 per cent per year.

Yet these facts are not uniquely the cause of the crisis in 1964. In a certain important sense they are not the cause at all. This may be seen by comparing the major components of the balance of payments for the three years which culminated in the 1955 balance-of-payments crisis and the three which culminated in the 1964 crisis. While the periods are not precisely comparable—the 1955 crisis occurred earlier in the year than did that in 1964—the difference in timing will not distort the general conclusions to be drawn from the comparison.

The most striking fact indicated by Table 3, which presents these data, is that the deterioration of Britain's balance of payments

TABLE 3

COMPONENTS OF THE BALANCE OF PAYMENTS
1953–55 AND 1962–64

	1953	1954	1955	1962	1963	1964	Average 1953–55	Average 1962–64	Change 1953–55 1962–64
Current transactions:									
Exports	(2683)	(2785)	(3073)	(3994)	(4287)	(4471)	(2847)	(4251)	(1404)
Imports	(2927)	(2989)	(3386)	(4092)	(4366)	(5005)	(3101)	(4488)	(1392)
Balance	−244	−204	−313	−98	−80	−534	−254	−237	+24
Invisibles, net	+395	+325	+156	+191	+184	+122	+292	+166	−126
Long-term capital:	(−194)	(−191)	(−122)	(−93)	(−162)	(−344)	(−169)	(−200)	(−31)
Official, net	−49	−28	−62	−104	−105	−116	−46	−108	−62
Other, net	−145	−163	−60	+11	−57	−228	−123	−91	+32
Balancing item	+26	+53	+123	+89	−68	+35	+67	+19	−48
Overall deficit (D) or surplus (S)	D 17	D 17	D 156	S 89	D 125	D 721	D 63	D 252	D 189

Source: Data for 1953–55, N.I.E.S.R. *Economic Review*, August, 1965, p. 74; data for 1962–64, data obtained before publication which will appear in *ibid.*, November, 1965, Table 14. For purposes of summing the columns to arrive at the overall deficit, figures in parentheses are duplicated by the figures below them and should be omitted. Small discrepancies in totals are caused by rounding.

from the 1950's to the 1960's is not due to a worsening of the trade position (nor to an increase in net private long-term investment abroad). The increasing trade deficit which one might expect from the export and import trends mentioned above has not appeared.

The explanation of the trade figures lies in the price trends of exports and imports. Export prices have risen by 1½ to 2 per cent per year during the 1953–64 period. As a result, the value of exports has risen by 1½ to 2 per cent per year faster than the physical volume of exports. Moreover, until 1962 not only were the prices of imports falling relative to the rising U.K. price level, they were falling absolutely, so that the value of imports rose by less than the physical volume. The upturn in import prices in 1963 and 1964 did not cause the trade balance to worsen relative to that for 1953–55; at most, it merely kept that balance from improving.

It is true that the swing from approximate balance in international receipts and payments as a whole in 1962 and 1963 to unprecedented deficit in 1964 was caused by an increase of more than 450 million pounds in the trade deficit from the 1962–63 average to 1964 and of about 200 million pounds in net private long-term investment abroad. (In part the latter increase was due to a reduction in American investment in Britain, which in 1962 and 1963 offset British investment abroad to a greater degree). Nevertheless, from the years 1953–55 to 1962–64, both the trade deficit and the total of net private long-term investment abroad *decreased,* because while they were unusually high in 1964 they were unusually low in 1962 and 1963.

Nevertheless, monetary reserves were not accumulated in 1962 and 1963. The main reason they were not was the increase in the government's net current expenditures and loans abroad. The data in millions of pounds are as follows:[10]

	Average 1953–55	Average 1962–64	Change
Government current receipts from abroad and expenditures to abroad:			
Debits (payments)	232	435	+203
Credits (receipts)	124	40	−84
Net receipts	−108	−394	−287
All other invisibles	+403	+560	+157

While the favorable annual balance of private current invisibles increased by 157 million pounds from 1953–55 to 1962–64, government credits fell by 84 million pounds and government debits rose by 203 million pounds. The increase in government current expenditures alone caused an added drain of 609 million pounds during the years 1962-64. In addition, as Table 3 shows, net government loans increased by 64 million pounds per year, or a total of 192 million pounds during the three-year period. (The increased drain of funds was much less, for much of the increase was in loans for economic aid, in large part respent in Britain.[11]) Without these increases in government current expenditures and loans, reserves in 1964 would have been ample to pay for the cyclical upsurge in imports.

The drain on the balance of payments which these expenditures abroad entailed was masked in 1962 and 1963 by the unusually favorable balance of trade and private investment. When imports and net private long-term investment abroad rose so much in 1964 that the trade deficit and net private long-term investment abroad for 1962–64 as a whole reached almost the magnitude of 1953–55, the mask was removed and the crisis of 1964 occurred.

In short, the severity of the balance-of-payments crisis of 1964–65 is due largely to the fact that other components of the balance of payments had not improved sufficiently to offset the increased governmental expenditures abroad required by the international responsibilities of Britain.

The increase in governmental expenditures abroad is not the only change within the "invisibles" group which caused a drain of funds. Some of the private expenditures items worsened. For example, as income rose in Britain, recorded tourist expenditures by Britons abroad increased more than did the tourist expenditures of foreigners in Britain. More important quantitatively, several sterling area countries experienced deficits in their own balances of payments and met them by drawing on their deposits in London. (These withdrawals were offset partly or wholly by increased deposits by several nonsterling area countries.) In addition to these recorded items, the shrinking of the balancing item by 43 million pounds per year (using the revised 1964 data) probably reflects an increase in unrecorded British tourist expenditures abroad, as well as some unrecorded speculative withdrawals late in 1964 and various other items.

That these are the causes of the crisis of 1964–65 has important implications for the future. An adverse balance of payments of or approaching the magnitude of the average deficit for 1962–64 is grave enough. However, prospects for the future would be even graver if forces were present that were tending to cause the deficit to increase steadily. But nothing in the forces that have operated during the past decade suggests a worsening trend.

First, with some reservations about the continuing effects of the Rhodesian declaration of independence, one may hope that the political conditions which have caused the increase in governmental expenditures abroad will not worsen. Second, the various economic factors which have caused deficits in the balances of payments of several sterling area countries, notably Australia, do not seem to contain within themselves seeds of further deterioration. While British tourist expenditures abroad, if unchecked, might continue to rise faster than expenditures of foreign tourists in Britain, tightened administration of regulations already in effect can readily curb the trend.

Above all, contrary to much recent analysis [12] there does not seem to be a worsening trend in the relation of imports to exports. During the past dozen years, while the physical volume of imports has risen at a faster rate than that of exports, the *value* of imports has not. The reason, as noted above, is that the prices of exports has been steadily rising, while until 1963 import prices had been falling. If income in Britain increases at a faster rate in future years than it has between 1953 and 1963, the rate of increase in imports will be higher. However, data on exports for 1963, 1964, and 1965, together with an increase in orders for ships and some heavy industrial products, suggest that the rate of increase in exports is also accelerating.

The physical volume of imports has increased as rapidly as it has, during the past dozen years, partly because the prices of imports have been falling relative to prices in Britain. If that price fall is resumed, after a reversal in 1963 and 1964, the value of imports will continue to rise less rapidly than the physical volume. If the relative fall in import prices ceases, then the physical volume may be expected to increase less rapidly than the past trend would suggest. For these reasons, the past trend in the *value* of imports appears to be a better guide to the future than their physical volume.[13] It therefore seems reasonable to assume that Britain's trade deficit (in the absence of successful governmental measures to reduce it) will remain at the 1962–64 level (or the 1953–55 level, which is approximately the same).

Let us consider what the balance of payments for a year of the period 1967–70 might be, on two assumptions: (1) that neither the restrictive measures of 1964–65 nor the measures to improve British economic performance had been instituted, and that the means to finance the deficit existed; and (2) that the restrictive measures had been retained during the period before the measures to improve economic performance had taken effect.

TABLE 4

HYPOTHETICAL UNRESTRICTED AND RESTRICTED BALANCE OF
PAYMENTS, 1967–70

(Millions of Pounds)

	Unrestricted	*Restricted*
Current transactions:		
Exports minus imports	−240	−140
"Invisibles," net:		
Services	−75	0
Transfers	−150	−150
Property income	+375	+375
Long-term capital movements:		
Official	−120 ⎫	
Other	−100 ⎬	−100
Balancing item	+60	+60
Overall balance	−250	+45

The hypothetical unrestricted balance differs from the average balance of 1962–64 mainly in that "transfers" to abroad (net withdrawals of short-term deposits) are assumed to be slightly larger and, with speculative withdrawals assumed to be zero, the balancing item is assumed to return to approximately its average for the past dozen years. Net transfers of funds are assumed to be larger because the increase over 1962–64 in withdrawals to meet adverse balance of payments is assumed to be greater than the increase in the inflow of deposits. Official long-term lending is held to its present level except for renewal of amortization of the American government loan.

The estimates of the restricted balance of payments are based on government intentions, experience to date, and judgments of feasibility. The reduction in the trade deficit results from continuation of the 10 per cent import surcharge and the reduction in long-term capital movements from severe administrative restriction on both government loans and private investment. (Continued deferment of payments on the American loan is also assumed.) The elimination of the deficit in service payments is assumed to be accomplished by tighter administration of limitations on tourist expenditures abroad, reduction in current government expenditures abroad, and continuation of purchases by Germany to offset the foreign exchange costs of maintaining the British armed forces in Germany. Even if these were not continued, or turned out to be merely financing of exports to Germany which would have been made in any event, there would be a slight balance-of-payments surplus.[14]

Thus, if these calculations are correct, payments and receipts can be balanced even if income and output are allowed to rise as fast as the increase in productive capacity permits. But balance attained by these means is not a condition to be contemplated with equanimity. Some of the restrictive measures now in effect can be maintained permanently if the balance-of-payments situation compels it. They do not do great economic harm. Perhaps this is true of restriction on government expenditures abroad; regulations to reduce the amount of money carried abroad by travelers, especially tourists, and to reduce the purchases of houses abroad and the like; and some of the regulations restricting the transfer of funds to abroad for investment and increasing the repatriation of receipts from sales of physical property or securities abroad.

However, continuation of other of the restrictive measures would be much more injurious both economically and politically. The surcharge on imports can hardly be retained indefinitely—nor should it be. There will be increasing pressure continuation of the present degree of control of the financing of private investment abroad, and for the most efficient operation of business it is desirable that that control should be relaxed as soon as possible. As long as the government must restrict its expenditures abroad as rigidly as at present, it will be crippled in its international political relations.

Further, even if all of Britain's present international debts were forgiven, the meager surplus in the balance of payments attained by the present restrictions—and with due allowance for error in the projections, the surplus attained by present restrictive measures will not be large—provides no margin for economic contingencies. If the rate of increase in world industrial production shrinks, the demand for Britain's exports will fall. To meet their own economic problems, countries holding deposits in London may withdraw them at an increased rate. Greater military expenditures abroad may be required. Even if none of these adverse developments occurs, another cyclical surge in imports will surely occur at some future period of accelerated rise in income. That period may not be far off.

Finally, of course the international debts will not be forgiven. They must be repaid. Repayment is now scheduled by 1970. Undoubtedly if Britain is making progress in meeting her economic problems, the payment schedule can be stretched out. But for the sake of international confidence it should not be stretched out far.

Britain's economic behavior must be altered so that a steady, dependable, continued improvement in the balance of payments occurs—one sufficient to create first a balance and then an increasing surplus when the restrictive measures now in force are removed. This must be the dominant objective of Britain's economic policy during the coming decade. Only one component in the balance of payments is susceptible to such a change in trend. While other changes can give temporary relief, the long-term remedy to Britain's balance-of-payments problem must consist of a change in the relative rate at which her exports and imports are increasing over time. The annual rate of increase in imports must be reduced, or that in exports increased. There is no other road to economic solvency.

The Policy Measures

Some of the measures adopted to increase exports have not been discussed above. First among these was formation of the British National Export Council late in 1964, to strive to increase exports by getting additional information about foreign markets, organizing export missions, promoting displays abroad of British products, and prodding British firms to increase their sales efforts and better adapt their products for foreign use and their procedures to foreign business practices. The B.N.E.C., initially financed by the government, in 1965 was raising funds from private firms to cover half of its annual budget of somewhat more than 200,000 pounds.

Many other measures and proposals followed. The coverage of credit insurance was increased and its cost halved. A list of about four hundred exporters "willing to help firms making complementary products to export" [15] was prepared and distributed widely. Proposals were discussed for export trading corporations, a national exporting organization to help small and medium-sized firms, and cooperative exporting by whole industries to prevent individual firms from fearing loss of home customers if they had too small output to serve both the home and foreign markets. In October, 1965, Lord Brown (Wilfrid Brown), known for his participation in the reorganization for greater efficiency of the industrial firm of Glacier Metals, Ltd., was appointed Joint Minister of State in the Board of Trade, with the assignment of administering these and other measures which might make British industry more "export-minded."

One may be skeptical of the results such measures will achieve. However, the men heading the efforts are competent industrial administrators, and if the introduction of the new measures coincides with a shift in British attitudes, the impact may be appreciable.

Early in June, 1965, a "little Neddy" was formed to attack a transport problem handicapping British exporters, the delays involved in achieving deliveries to abroad. It was charged with making proposals for changes in goods handling methods to speed the movement of exports from manufacturer to foreign and especially continental customers. Lord Caldecote, managing director of the guided missiles division of the British Aircraft Corporation, was made its chairman. It has as one member the head of the National Ports Council, already charged with proposals for the improvement of port facilities and methods, but its scope is much wider than the scope of that body. The council promptly began the study of five projects: inland clearance depots, the roll-on roll-off system, the use of standardized containers, permitting general access to docks, and simplifying shipping documentation.

Considerations cited in an article in the *Economist* (June 5, 1965) indicated the possibility of practical improvement:

> At the end of 1964, the Federation of British Industries has estimated for D.E.A., there were two weeks' more export deliveries in the pipeline than at the beginning of the year; that could represent a pretty significant element in the visible trade balance. . . . Responsibility for outward movement, in many

groups [of companies], rests with a traffic manager who is
fairly junior in the hierarchy; how the goods get abroad once
they leave the factory is a matter that never gets up to main
board level. Questions like the widespread use of roll on roll
off transport across the Channel and North Sea, 'containerisa-
tion', and other elements in the intelligent purchasing of movement facilities may never get the attention—or decisions—
that they need.

In creating this little Neddy, D.E.A. is drawing upon the
experience mainly of Northern Ireland. . . . Companies such
as Gallahers have been able to cut down some average delivery periods from three weeks to about 36 hours—and reduce
pilferage almost to nil. . . . The department has also been
looking at the experience of the Danes and the Swedes in
putting on specialized ships to handle trade with Britain—
and over and above the possibilities of making sea travel more
efficient, at air freight.

The changes being studied now have been proposed before. The
strong resistance of dock unions has been a major obstacle to the
adoption of some of them. However, if a revolution in dock practices is achieved through the decasualization of labor and related
changes proposed in the Devlin report, concomitant introduction
of some of the changes being studied by the "little Neddy" may be
possible. As in the case of the foreign sales methods of British firms,
achieving these improvements in shipping methods will depend more
on changes in attitudes than on fresh analysis of proposals. One of
the relevant changes in attitude is that within the government: the
Labour government now in power displays both a firmer will to
overcome labor resistances to change and greater resourcefulness in
doing so than any previous government of recent decades. But this
change will not be enough unless there is also some change in the
spirit of the dock unions.

While the measures to spur exports were being developed, the
"little Neddy" of each industry was asked to analyze the possibility
of increased production or improvements in products within that
industry that would reduce imports. Early attention was focused
on possibilities in chemicals, machine tools, and mechanical engineering products. In each of these fields imports have risen greatly.
Publicity concerning specific imported manufactures of all types was

given by a 1965 publication of the National Economic Development ment Council, *Imported Manufactures: An Inquiry into Competitiveness.* Few specific measures have been undertaken other than this pubilicity and the prodding which individual "little Neddies" may be doing within their industries—but of course these actions may have some effect.

The Prospects for Success

Yet measures directed at specific inadequacies in competing with foreign producers seem much less significant than the comprehensive attack on price rises and on the barriers to an increased rate of advance in productivity in every industry. If these measures cause—or permit—a steady continuing increase in the ability of British producers to compete with the producers of other industrial countries, then the attempt to restore the balance of payments to health will succeed. If they do not cause this cumulative improvement, the attempt will fail. Of course this unqualified generalization is an overstatement, for success will be determined by the combined result of all of the varied measures now being pushed forward. But the overstatement is slight: the attack on inflation and the attempt to accelerate the increase in productivity throughout industry are together the keystone of the arch.

Whether they will succeed, no one can now tell. Between the lines of this essay, the reader may have read the writer's subjective judgment that they will. Or, more correctly, the judgment is that the change in the temper of the British nation, supplemented by these measures of a government itself reflecting the new temper, will succeed. But that judgment is so subjective, so little based on overt empirical evidence, that it must be termed merely intuitive.

If the putative change in national temper plus the measures which collectively form the "national plan" do not bring success, then devaluation (one devaluation, not a series decade after decade) may restore economic balance. It may do so, that is, provided that confidence in London as a world financial center survives it. But devaluation would be a petty end to an enterprise that has elements of grandeur. Anyone who has informed himself on the national economic effort sufficiently to sense its high drama must hope that it will succeed.

Notes

I. The Tide Begins to Rise

1. One measure of local control not used before the war was retained. This was the requirement that a firm wishing to build a factory or an addition to one, beyond a certain size, even in an area zoned for industry, must obtain an Industrial Development Certificate. The purpose presumably was to prevent urban congestion, and perhaps also to divert industry to areas where unemployment was a problem.

2. Quoted in Samuel Brittan, *The Treasury under the Tories, 1951–1964* (London: Penguin, 1964), p. 187.

3. The measurement of unemployment differs in the two countries. On balance, some individuals are counted as unemployed in the United States who are not included in Britain. Thus when British records show unemployment of 2 per cent, if the American concepts had been used, the percentage derived in precisely the same circumstances might have been, say, 3 per cent or possibly 3½ per cent. (These figures are illustrative; it is impossible to know the precise percentage differences which would result.) However, the statement in the text holds true with maximum allowance for this difference in the unemployment concepts in the two countries.

4. In considering these data, it should be noted that the indexes of export prices are inexact. Exports are heterogeneous and any set of weights used to derive an index of their prices is somewhat unrepresentative. However, there is no obvious reason to expect systematic bias in either direction in any country relative to any other.

5. Committee on the Working of the Monetary System, *Report* (Radcliffe Report) (London: H.M.S.O., 1959 [Cmnd. 827]), especially Ch. 6.

II. New Viewpoints

1. The account here of this dining club and the participation of its members in the F.B.I. discussion group in economic growth is from Brittan, pp. 216–18.

2. Michael Shanks, "The Mid-Year Outlook," F.B.I. *Review,* June, 1961, pp. 31–36.

3. See the following essays: R. G. Lipsey, "The Relation between Unemployment and the Rate of Change of Money Wage Rates in the United Kingdom, 1862–1957: A Further Analysis," *Economica,* Vol. 27, 1960, pp. 1–31; L. Dicks-Mireaux, "The Interrelationship between Cost and Price Changes, 1946–1959: A Study of Inflation in Postwar Britain," *Oxford Economic Papers,* Vol. 13, 1961, pp. 267–92; A. W. Phillips, "The Relation between Unemployment and the Rate of Money Wage Rates in the United Kingdom, 1861–1957," *Economica,* Vol. 25, 1958, pp. 283–99, and "Employment, Inflation and Growth," *Economica,* Vol. 29, 1962, pp. 1–16; F. W. Paish, *Studies in an Inflationary Economy* (London: Macmillan, 1962); see also Brittan, pp. 208 and 289–94, for a discussion of the circulation of a similar doctrine within the Treasury.

4. William J. Fellner, *et al., The Problem of Rising Prices* (Paris: O.E.E.C., 1961).

III. REORGANIZATION OF THE CONTROL OF GOVERNMENT EXPENDITURES

1. P. D. Henderson, "Government and Industry," in G. D. N. Worswick and P. H. Ady, eds., *The British Economy in the 1950's* (London: Oxford University Press, 1963), p. 374.

2. Brittan states that it was first made explicit in 1884 (Brittan, p. 80).

3. Between 1954 and 1960 public expenditures rose by 20 per cent, while gross domestic product rose by 18 per cent.

4. *Control of Public Expenditure* (Plowden Report) (London: H.M.S.O., 1961 [Cmnd. 1432]).

5. Precise limits, if they exist, have not been made public. The figures are from Brittan, p. 84.

IV. THE FORMATION OF THE NATIONAL ECONOMIC DEVELOPMENT COUNCIL

1. A few smaller unions have not joined the T.U.C. Any union may be expelled for conduct deemed injurious to the interests of the labor movement as a whole.

2. Mr. Lloyd stated this in an article, "NEDDY and Parliament," *Crossbow,* October–December, 1963. For a discussion of his attitude, see Brittan, pp. 219–21.

3. Repeatedly in later issues the *Economist* returned to the theme. The most urgently needed function of the council, the periodical stated on November 18, would be to persuade the government to take such

actions as to close inefficient industries, abandon protection, resist strikes, and introduce distinct wage differentials. Few other newspapers or periodicals put the issue quite so clearly.

4. Brittan, p. 212.

V. THE FUNCTIONING OF THE NATIONAL ECONOMIC DEVELOPMENT COUNCIL

1. National Economic Development Council, *History and Functions* (London: N.E.D.C., 1962; mimeographed).

2. By and large the agency under a minister is termed a department. In ministries which serve several administratively distinct functions there is more than one department, and in some, such as the Board of Trade, the term department is not applied. The term ministry is used when one is visualizing the minister and his policies; the word department is used in most other references.

3. The National Building Agency was established in 1964 to provide information to local authorities concerning the construction methods being offered by various builders, to do research, and by both activities to influence construction methods. The forerunner of the coordinated contract-letting scheme is CLASP, the Consortium of Local Authorities Special Programme, which for more than a decade has been organizing groups of education authorities into consortia for bulk ordering of components for school buildings. The volume of housing construction by local authorities is some ten times as great as that of schools. See "Houses, Fast," *Economist,* May 29, 1965.

VII. THE LABOUR GOVERNMENT'S QUIET REVOLUTION IN PLANNING

1. F. T. Blackaby, "The United Kingdom: The New Pattern of Economic Administration" (mimeographed), p. 32.

2. Cmnd. 2764.

3. Cmnd. 2734.

4. *Third Report* of the Estimates Committee, Session 1964–65 (House of Commons Paper No. 273).

5. *Machinery of a Prices and Income Policy* (London: H.M.S.O., 1965 [Cmnd. 2577]).

VIII. REGIONAL, LOCAL, AND TRANSPORTATION PLANNING

1. Scottish Development Council, *Report of the Local Development Committee* (Carncross Report) (Edinburgh: H.M.S.O., 1950).

2. National Economic Development Council, *Conditions Favourable to Faster Growth* (London: H.M.S.O., 1963).

3. *South East England* (London: H.M.S.O., 1964 [Cmnd. 2308]).

4. The *Economist* suggested that in order to counteract the attractions of London the administrative capital of Britain should be transferred to the north of the country.

IX. PLANNING IN FRANCE: A FRAME OF REFERENCE

1. The account presented here is based primarily on J. and A. M. Hackett, *Economic Planning in France* (London: Allen & Unwin, 1963); Michel Crozier, "General Outline of a Depth Study on French Planning Methods," a paper given at the Minnowbrook Conference on Action under the sponsorship of the Comparative Administration Group (American Society for Public Administration) and the Maxwell Graduate School of Citizenship and Public Affairs, Syracuse University, July, 1964 (mimeographed); and Andrew Shonfield, *Modern Capitalism: The Changing Balance of Public and Private Power* (London: Oxford University Press, 1965), Chs. 5–10, of which Mr. Shonfield kindly sent the manuscript to the authors.

For briefer accounts, see also an essay by Bernard Cazes in Organisation for Economic Co-operation and Development, *Report of an International Trade Union Seminar on Economic and Social Programming, Paris 1964* (Paris: O.E.C.D., 1964); and M. MacLennan, *French Planning: Some Lessons for Britain* (London: Political and Economic Planning, 1963).

2. The Conseil Supérieur or High Planning Commission is a much smaller superior body. Many of its members participate in the planning process described below, and therefore in general approve the plan as it is drawn up. This is one main reason why it has not seemed necessary to refer the completed plan to the Conseil Supérieur.

3. J. and A. M. Hackett, Appendix III. We present this information concerning the commissions and working parties for the fourth and fifth plans rather than the third simply because we do not have detailed data for the third. The principles of composition were the same.

4. In the process, use is made of national accounts for the final year of the plan estimated by the Services des Etudes Economiques et Financières (S.E.E.F.) of the Ministry of Finance; investment and labor requirements estimated by the horizontal commissions, supplemented by detailed industry studies by such organizations as B.I.P.E. (Bureau d'Information et des Prévisions Economiques); income elasticities of

demand, as calculated by C.R.E.D.O.C. (Centre des Recherches Economiques et de Documentations sur la Consommation); and the input-
output tables of I.N.S.E.E. (Institut National de Statistiques et Etudes
Economiques). The process is neatly summarized in C. P. Kindleberger,
"French Planning," a paper prepared for a Universities National Bureau
Conference on Economic Planning held at Princeton, N.J., on November
27, 28, 1964.

5. J. and A. M. Hackett, foreword by M. Massé, p. 8.

6. Shonfield, Ch. 7.

7. Shonfield, Ch. 7.

8. This figure excludes housing construction.

9. *Fonds de Développement Économique et Social* (Seventh Report),
cited by MacLennan.

10. This statement, from the official text of the fourth plan, is quoted
by Shonfield, Ch. 8.

11. Shonfield, Ch. 7.

12. Cited by C. P. Kindleberger in Hoffmann, *et al., In Search of
France,* (Cambridge: Harvard University Press, 1963), p. 153.

X. BRITISH PLANNING AND BRITISH CHARACTER

1. Stanley Hoffmann, "Paradoxes of the French Political Community," in Hoffmann, *et al., In Search of France,* pp. 1–117.

2. See Crozier, "General Outline of a Depth Study on French Planning Methods."

3. This statement by P. D. Henderson, quoted in Ch. III, that differences among government departments are settled by a "process of quasi-
diplomatic negotiation" and not entirely by the determination of social
priorities, amounts to a statement that this principle applies within
government. At the psychoanalytical level, it is possible that jostling
among individuals without any clear criterion for the resolution of the
friction arouses a degree of (unconscious) alarm in Britons that it does
not among, say, Frenchmen or Americans, and that this is the explanation of the fact that Britons are more inhibited about such jostling.

Perhaps it is not fanciful to suppose that one of the attractions of
empire to Britons has been that it provided a channel in which to vent
vigorously and boldly the power which one could use only with circumspection at home.

4. Where there is a degree of consultation and common understanding between government administrators and business leaders concerning governmental policy, it is often difficult to know who is regulating

whom. No implication of subservience by either government or business is intended. The situation is much more complex than this. But it is certainly not one of *laissez faire*.

5. Shonfield states this principle of the freedom of spontaneous association in British society and discusses it at some length.

XI. WILL PLANNING SUCCEED?

1. E. L. Trist, G. W. Higgin, H. Murray, and A. B. Pollock, *Organizational Choice: Capabilities of Groups at the Coal Face under Changing Technologies* (London: Tavistock Publications, 1963).

2. Tom Burns, "What Managers Do," *New Society,* December 17, 1964, pp. 8–9.

3. See William Rees-Mogg, "The Changemakers," *Sunday Times,* March 7, 1965.

4. A Conservative Political Research Center Pamphlet, "Efficiency and Beyond," March 1965, quoted in the *Sunday Times,* March 14, 1965.

5. See Table 1, p. 6 above, and the *Economic Report of the President,* transmitted to the Congress, January, 1965 (Washington: G.P.O., 1965). The calculated difference in rate of increase in output per worker in the two countries depends on the beginning and terminal years selected. If 1954 and 1964, years of approximately the same percentage of unemployment, are used for the United States, the calculated difference is about ¼ per cent. With due allowance for a margin of error because of the effect of slack in the American economy, the "true" difference can hardly be as great as ½ per cent, and may be much less than ¼ per cent.

6. There may have been much larger speculative withdrawals, offset in part by an inflow of funds attracted by the high interest rates that could be earned in London.

7. The estimated division between net payments for services and net withdrawals of short-term funds is that estimated by the National Institute of Economic and Social Research on the basis of the May 1965 estimates of the two combined for 1964, roughly adjusted by me to agree with the September revisions. See N.I.E.S.R., *Economic Review* August, 1965, p. 14.

8. The reactions of individuals in E.F.T.A. countries to the surcharge on imports was irrational from a purely economic viewpoint. It was necessary for Britain to reduce imports. Quantitative controls, which were permitted under E.F.T.A. rules, were impossible, the machinery did not exist. Deflation within the British economy sufficient to achieve

the necessary reduction in imports would have reduced the sales of foreign producers as a group to Britain by as much as did the surcharge and, unless E.F.T.A. members expected favorably discriminatory treatment, would presumably have reduced theirs by as much, though of course the distribution of the effect among countries might have been different. That it is proper for Britain to suffer unnecessarily if other countries must suffer is not logical. The intensity of the reaction of leaders in the other E.F.T.A. countries is perhaps explained by the fact that all of those economies are small relative to that of Britain and the exports of all to Britain are large relative both to their total exports and to their national income. Their helplessness in the face of unilateral action by a large partner may be the explanation of an excessive reaction.

9. See the calculation presented in the *Economist,* September 18, 1965, p. 1135. The estimate of speculative or semispeculative withdrawals of 400 million pounds is also presented there.

10. For 1962–64 data see *Financial Statistics,* October, 1965, p. 94. The data for 1953–55 were provided by N.I.E.S.R.

11. Of course, they reduced the volume of British production available for use in Britain.

12. For a solidly based piece of research which nevertheless seems to this writer to be erroneous, see the discussion of "The Economic Situation" in N.I.E.S.R., *Economic Review,* August, 1965, especially pp. 15–21.

13. In economic terms, it is more reasonable to assume that the price elasticity of demand for imports is unity rather than zero. Indeed, since many of the imports are fairly close substitutes for British products, the most plausible assumption is that the elasticity of demand is greater than unity.

14. The effect of the 1965 tax changes on the remittance to Britain of the profits of subsidiaries abroad is assumed to be offset by the increased pressure to finance investment abroad out of those earnings. The balancing item is assumed to remain unaffected by the restrictive measures because the curtailment of illegal transfers of funds to abroad by tourists is assumed to be offset by the increased pressure for illegal tranfers caused by other restrictions.

15. *National Plan,* p. 72.

‡‡‡‡‡‡‡‡‡‡‡‡‡‡‡‡‡‡‡‡‡‡‡‡‡‡‡‡‡‡‡‡ ‡‡‡‡‡‡‡‡‡‡‡‡‡‡‡‡‡‡‡‡‡‡‡‡‡‡‡‡‡‡‡

Selected Bibliography

BRITISH PLANNING

Government Documents

Central Statistical Office. *National Income and Expenditure.* . . . **Annual** volumes, 1960–64. London: H.M.S.O.

Committee of Inquiry into Dock Labour. *Report.* (Devlin Report.) London: H.M.S.O., 1965. (Cmnd. 2734)

Committee of Inquiry into the Organization of Civil Science. *Report.* (Trend Report.) London: H.M.S.O., 1963. (Cmnd. 2171)

Committee on the Working of the Monetary System. *Report.* (Radcliffe Report.) London: H.M.S.O., 1959. (Cmnd. 827)

Control of Public Expenditure. (Plowden Report.) London: H.M.S.O., 1961. (Cmnd. 1432)

Council on Prices, Productivity, and Incomes. *First [Second, Third, Fourth] Report.* London: H.M.S.O., 1958 [1958, 1959, 1961].

The Financial and Economic Obligations of the Nationalised Industries. London: H.M.S.O., 1961. (Cmnd. 1337)

Incomes Policy: The Next Step. London: H.M.S.O., 1962.

Land Commission. London: H.M.S.O., 1965. (Cmnd. 2771)

Machinery of a Price and Incomes Policy. London: H.M.S.O., 1965. (Cmnd. 2577)

National Economic Development Council. "History and Functions." London: N.E.D.C., 1962 (mimeographed).

———. *Conditions Favourable to Faster Growth.* London: H.M.S.O., 1963.

———. *Export Trends.* London: H.M.S.O., 1963.

———. *Growth of the United Kingdom Economy, 1961–66.* London: H.M.S.O., 1963.

———. *The Construction Industry.* London: H.M.S.O., 1964.

———. *Growth of the Economy.* London: H.M.S.O., 1964.

———. *Imported Manufacturers: An Inquiry into Competitiveness.* London: H.M.S.O., 1965.

National Plan. London: H.M.S.O., 1965. (Cmnd. 2764)

The North East: A Programme for Regional Development and Growth. London: H.M.S.O., 1963. (Cmnd. 2206)

Public Expenditure in 1963–64 and 1967–68. London: H.M.S.O., 1963. (Cmnd. 2235)

Public Investment in Britain. London: H.M.S.O., 1960. (Cmnd. 1203)

Scottish Development Council. *Central Scotland: A Programme for Development and Growth.* Edinburgh: H.M.S.O., 1963. (Cmnd. 2188)

————. *Report of the Local Development Committee.* (Cairncross Report.) Edinburgh: H.M.S.O., 1950.

South East England. London: H.M.S.O., 1964. (Cmnd. 2308)

Third Report [of the Estimates Committee, Session 1964–65]. (House of Commons Paper, No. 273) London: H.M.S.O., 1965.

Traffic in Towns. (Reports of the Steering Group and Working Group Appointed by the Ministry of Transport.) London: H.M.S.O., 1963.

Treasury Control of Expenditure. (Sixth Report of the [Parliamentary] Select Committee on Estimates.) London: H.M.S.O., 1958.

Books

Brittan, Samuel. *The Treasury under the Tories, 1951–1964.* London: Penguin Books, 1964.

Business Economists Group. *Planning.* (Report of Oxford Conference.) 1962. Obtainable from 21 Godliman Street, London, E.C.4.

Dow, J. C. R. *The Management of the British Economy, 1945–60.* London: Cambridge University Press, 164.

Fellner, William J., *et al. The Problem of Rising Prices.* Paris: O.E.E.C., 1961.

Flanders, Allan. *The Fawley Productivity Agreements.* London: Faber, 1964.

Kindleberger, Charles P. *Economic Growth in France and Britain, 1851–1950.* Cambridge (Mass.): Harvard University Press, 1964.

London and Cambridge Economic Service. *The British Economy: Key Statistics, 1900–1964.* London: 1965.

Maddison, Angus. *Economic Growth in the West.* New York: Twentieth Century Fund, 1964.

Organisation for European Economic Co-operation. See Fellner.

Paish, F. W. *Studies in an Inflationary Economy.* London: Macmillan Co., 1962.

Political and Economic Planning. *Growth in the British Economy.* London: P.E.P., 1960.

————. *Thrusters and Sleepers.* London: P.E.P., 1965.

Sampson, A. *Anatomy of Britain.* London: Hodder & Stoughton, 1962.

Scott, M. F. *A Study of United Kingdom Imports.* Cambridge: Cambridge University Press, 1963.

Shonfield, Andrew. *British Economic Policy since the War*. London: Penguin Books, 1959.

——. *Modern Capitalism: The Changing Balance of Public and Private Power*. London: Oxford University Press, 1965.

Trist, E. L., G. W. Higgin, H. Murray, and A. B. Pollock. *Organizational Choice: Capabilities of Groups at the Coal Face under Changing Technologies*. London: Tavistock Publications, 1963.

Worswick, G. D. N., and P. H. Ady, eds. *The British Economy, 1945–50*. London: Oxford University Press, 1952.

——. *The British Economy in the 1950's*. London: Oxford University Press, 1963.

Articles

Blackaby, F. T. "The United Kingdom: The New Pattern of Economic Administration" [n.d.] (mimeographed).

Burns, Tom. "What Managers Do." *New Society*, December 17, 1964, pp. 8–9.

Dicks-Mireaux, L. "The Interrelationship between Cost and Price Changes, 1946–1959: A Study of Inflation in Post-War Britain." *Oxford Economic Papers*, Vol. 13, 1961, pp. 267–92.

Lipsey, R. G. "The Relation between Unemployment and the Rate of Change of Money Wage Rates in the United Kingdom, 1862–1957: A Further Analysis." *Economica*, Vol. 27, 1960, pp. 1–31.

Neild, Robert. "New Functions, New Men?" *The Listener*, August 27, 1964, pp. 302–04.

Oppenheimer, P. M. "External Finance and the Balance of Payments." *Times Review of Industry and Technology* (London & Cambridge Bulletin, No. 54), June, 1965, pp. viii–xii.

Phillips, A. W. "The Relation between Unemployment and the Rate of Change of Money Wage Rates in the United Kingdom, 1861–1957." *Economica*, Vol. 25, 1958, pp. 283–99.

——. "Employment, Inflation, and Growth." *Economica*, Vol. 29, 1962, pp. 1–16.

Rees-Mogg, William. "The Changemakers." *Sunday Times*, March 7, 1965.

Reddaway, W. B. "Suspended Judgment." *Times Review of Industry and Technology* (London & Cambridge Bulletin, No. 54), June, 1965, pp. i–vii.

Shanks, Michael. "The Mid-Year Outlook." *F.B.I. Review*, June, 1961, pp. 31–36.

French Planning

André, René P. "Government Action and French Exports." Cambridge (Mass.): Massachusetts Institute of Technology, 1964. Unpublished thesis for M.S. degree (mimeographed).

Bauchet, Pierre. *Priorièté Publique et Planification.* Revised edition. Paris, Cujas, 1962 (first edition, 1958).

————. *Economic Planning: The French Experience.* Translation of the revised [1962] French edition. New York: Frederick A. Praeger, 1964.

Baum, W. C. *The French Economy and the State.* Princeton: Princeton University Press, 1958.

Cazes, Robert. "French Planning." In Organisation for Economic Co-operation and Development, *Report of an International Trade Union Seminar on Economic and Social Programming, Paris, 1964.* Paris: O.E.C.D., 1964.

Centre Européen pour le Progrès Economique et Social. *French and Other National Economic Plans for Growth.* Report of a conference held under the auspices of the French group in Paris, June, 1962. Distributed in the United States by the Committee on Economic Development, Washington, D.C., June 1963.

Crozier, Michel. "General Outline of a Depth Study on French Planning Methods." Paper given at the Minnowbrook Seminar, Conference on Action under Development Plans, held under the sponsorship of the Comparative Administration Group (American Society for Public Administration) and the Maxwell Graduate School of Citizenship and Public Affairs, Syracuse University, July, 1964 (mimeographed).

De Gaulle, Charles, President. "President De Gaulle Holds Eighth Press Conference." Ambassade de France, *Speeches and Press Conferences,* No. 192, July 29, 1963.

Dessau, Jan. "Incomes Planning and Policy: Recent French Experience and Analysis." Paper presented at the International Seminar in Economics of Labour and Industrial Relations, Ditchley Park, April, 1964 (mimeographed).

Hackett, John, and Anne-Marie Hackett. *Economic Planning in France.* London: Allen & Unwin, 1963.

Hoffmann, Stanley. "Paradoxes of the French Political Community." In Stanley Hoffmann, *et al., In Search of France.* Cambridge (Mass.): Harvard University Press, 1963, pp. 1–117.

Kindleberger, Charles P. "French Planning." Paper prepared for Universities National Bureau Conference on Economic Planning held at Princeton, N.J., November 27, 28, 1964.

————. "The Postwar Resurgence of the French Economy." In Stanley Hoffmann, *et al., In Search of France*. Cambridge (Mass.): Harvard University Press, 1963.

MacLennan, M. "French Planning: Some Lessons for Britain." *Planning* (P.E.P.), Vol. 29, No. 475, 1963.

Marczewski, J. "The Fourth French Plan (1962–1965): 'Conjuncture' and Planned Development." *Economie Appliquée,* Vol. 15, Nos. 1–2, June, 1962.

Massé, Pierre. "French Economic Planning." Address given at a symposium organized by the National Institute of Economic and Social Research, London, April 22, 1961. Ambassade de France, *French Affairs,* No. 127, December 1961.

Political and Economic Planning. "Economic Planning in France." *Planning,* Vol. 28, No. 454, 1961.

Sheahan, John. *Promotion and Control of Industry in Postwar France.* Cambridge (Mass.): Harvard University Press, 1963.

Shonfield, Andrew. *Modern Capitalism: The Changing Balance of Public and Private Power*. London: Oxford University Press, 1965.

Swann, D., and D. L. McLachlan. "Programming and Competition in the European Communities." *Economic Journal,* Vol. 74, No. 293, 1964.

Wellisz, S. "Economic Planning in the Netherlands, France and Italy." *Journal of Political Economy,* Vol. 68, No. 3, 1960.

Wickham, S. "French Planning: Retrospect and Prospect." *Review of Economics and Statistics,* Vol. 45, No. 4, 1963.

Index

Agriculture Ministry, 50
Amory, Heathcoat, 3
Association of British Manufacturers, 60
Aviation Ministry, 50

Balance of Payments: 2, 8, 9, 22–23, 88, 105, 143–145; goals, 67; exports, 68. *See also* Chancellor of the Exchequer
Balogh, Thomas, 63
Bank loans: control, 10
Bank of Canada, 144
Bank of England, 2, 144, 146–47, 150–55, 158–59
Bank Rate, 9, 10, 149
Banque de France, 108, 116
Barlow Report (White Paper on regional problems, 1938), 90
Beaver, Hugh (Sir), 17
Birch, Alan, 14
Board for Prices and Incomes, 136
Board of Trade, 42, 90, 98, 114, 125–26, 160
Bond market (Paris), 108
Boyle, Edward (Sir), 36
British Employers' Confederation, 35, 60
British Iron and Steel Federation, 20
British Transport Commission, 13
Brown, George, 62, 64–65, 76, 77, 79, 80–85, 97, 160
Budget (1959), 9
Bureaucracy, French, 117–18
Bureau d'Information et des Prévisions Economiques (B.I.P.E.), 166
Butler, R. A., 3
Butler revolution, 19
Butskellism, 3

Caisse des Dépôts et des Consignations, 107–08, 116

Caldecote (Lord), 160
Callaghan, 84
Candle-ends rule, 27–28
Cartelization, 111, 123, 141
Catherwood, H. F. R., 76–77, 136
Cement industry, 138
Cement Makers' Federation, 139
Chancellor of Exchequer, on balance of payments, 2, 151
"Command economy," 15
Commissariat Général du Plan de Modernisation et d'Équipement (*Commissariat au Plan*), 103–10, 113, 118–19
Commissions de Modernisation, 103, 113
Common Market: advantages in joining, 8–9, 34; 104
Confederation of British Industry, 80, 85–87
Conservative government, 18, 20, 40, 71, 72–75, 80, 94–95, 125, 127, 129, 144
Conservative party: 3, 14, 15, 122; and maximum employment, 4; attack on Wilson's speech, 18; and social justice, 19, 27; attitude toward planning, 35; policy, 45; on intervention, 125
Conservative Political Research Centre, 135
Consortium of Local Authorities Special Programme (CLASP), 165
Council on Prices, Productivity, and Incomes (C.O.P.P.A.I.): 13, 21–22; wage control, 23
Crosland, Anthony, 18
Customs and Excise Department, 23

Defence Minister, 147
De Gaulle, Charles, 103, 105, 113, 115

Demand: consumer goods, 11; long-term forecasts for five industries, 17; improvements in forecasting, 19, 76
Department of Economic Affairs: 30, 63, 65, 98, 112–13, 136; taking over functions from N.E.D.C., 78
Development Council, 126
Development District, 92
Dewdney, Duncan, 81, 136
Distribution of Industry Act of 1945, 90
Domestic production, 67

Economic Affairs, Ministry, 32, 62, 74, 87, 126
Economic analysis: machinery for, 12
Economic Development Committees: 48; formation of, 49. *See also* Little Neddies
Economic Planning Advisory Council, 51
Economic and Social Council, 113
Economic and Social Development Fund. *See Fonds de Développement Économique et Social*
Employment, 3, 4, 8, 14, 21, 45, 131
Exchange rate, 4
Expansionists, 3
Exports: rise in, 7; market difficulties, 24; survey of trends criticized, 47; French, 104; trading corporation, 160; prices, 163

Federation of British Industries (F.B.I.): 10, 13, 160; conference of, 17, 19, 43, 59
Finance Ministry (French), 108, 110
Fiscal measures: 2, 3; restrictive measures, 8; policy, 21. *See also* Butskellism
Fonds de Développement Économique et Social, 106, 107, 117
Fraser, Tom, 77.

Gaitskell, Hugh: 3; on National Income Commission, 55
Governmental intervention, 12, 21, 120–27

Governmental ownership, 121
Government Training Centers, 71
Growth rate, reasons for slow rise, 15
Gunter, Ray, 73

Henderson, P. D., 24
Housing and Local Government Ministry, 50, 94, 114

Imperative planning, 110
Imperial Chemical Industries, 93
Implementation of plans, 114
Imports: French, 104; trends, 153; volume, 156; value, 157
Incentives, 106
Indicative planning, 16, 68, 110, 137
Industrial Development Certificate, to control drift to the South, 91, 163
Industrial Estates, 97–98
Industrial Training Act of 1964, 141
Inflation: 3, 21–23, 60, 69, 88, 104; pressures, 129, 131
International Monetary Fund, 3, 150
Institute of Directors, 17
Investment programs: 18, 33; France, 109; private, 158

Jay, Douglas, 18
Jones, Aubrey, 80

Kaldor, Nicholas, 63
Keynesian theory, 2–3

Labour government, 2, 50, 67, 69, 70, 84, 87, 94, 95, 97, 101, 122–29, 136, 143, 144, 146, 149, 161
Labour Minister, 86
Labour Ministry: 56, 114; French, 110
Labour party: 1, 3, 14, 15, 29, 95, 132, 144, 149; attitude toward planning, 35–36; economic policy, 62; election pledges, 94; on intervention, 125, 127
Laissez faire, 122
Land Commission: 1965 White Paper on, 95, 96
Lating, J. M., 36

Lawrence, Geoffrey, Q.C., 55
Little Neddies: 64, 77–78, 113, 141–142, 160–61; for individual industries, 48; why delayed, 50; coverage, 51. See also Economic Development Committees
Lloyd, Selwyn, 22–23, 30, 35, 46
Local Employment Act, 90

MacDougall, Donald, 63–64
Macmillan, Harold: 3, 33; on Maudling's Budget, 57. See also Butskellism
Manpower Committee, 82
Marquand, Hilary, 81
Marshall Plan, 102
Masse, Pierre M., 105, 111, 114
Maudling, Reginald, 19, 45–46, 57
Monetary movement, 145
Monetary regulation, 2–3
Monetary system, Committee on the Working of, 10. See also Radcliffe Committee
Monnet, Jean, 118

National Association of British Manufacturers, 35
National Board for Prices and Incomes, 80, 84, 85, 86, 87, 88, 125
National Coal Board: rate of return, 31
National Economic Development Board, 126
National Economic Development Council (N.E.D.C.): 8–9, 20, 30, 33, 43, 46, 60–66, 89, 101–02, 112, 162; establishment proposed, 24; membership, 37, 39–40; operations, 50–52; on measures to increase productivity, 68; on conditions for faster growth, 91; on imports, 162
National Economy Group, 29–30
National Export Council, 159
National Incomes Commission: 30, 47, 53–54, 62, 80; Incomes Review Division, 80, 84, 87, 89; membership, 55; functioning of, 56; trade union reaction, 57; wage increases, 59; Prices Review division, 80
National Institute of Economic and Social Research: 10, 13, 15, 19; 1961 conference, 36, 44; criticism of N.I.C., 57
National Insurance: contributions, 10, 23
Nationalized industries: policies of, 30; French, 107
Nationalization policy: steel, 87; land, 96, 122
National Joint Advisory Council, 126
National Plan (White Paper), 64, 77, 100
National Ports Council, 160
National Production Advisory Council, 126
National Union of Railwaymen, 94–95
Neild, Robert, 32, 63
New Deal: mentioned, 143

Organization of European Economic Co-operation, 22–23
Overseas Development Ministry, 63

"Pay pause," 24
Phelps-Brown, E. H., 36
Plowden Committee, 13, 27–30
Powell, Enoch, 61
Prices: 4–5, 9, 20, 24, 110; stability, 22, 81, 84, 132
Private associations, 124
Private economy, 15
Private sector: French, 107
Production: rate of increase, 5; industrial, 10
Productivity, 9, 18, 33, 68, 69, 132, 135–37, 140
Public expenditures: and planning, 12, 27; Committee on Control of, 13; evaluation, 28. See also Plowden Committee
Public investment, 3, 9
Public policies: machinery for, 26
Public Works and Building Ministry, 50, 56, 114

Radcliffe Committee, 10, 12

Rearmament, 2
Regional development, 125
Regulation of the economy, short-run, 23
Renault automobile company, 106
Revolution of 1870, 115
Robertson, Dennis (Sir), 21
Royal Economic Society, 57
Rueff, Jacques, 105

Science and Education Ministry, 114
Scottish Building Employers' Federation, 56
Scottish Development Council, 90
Select Committee on Estimates, 13, 27, 76
Services des Etudes Economiques et Financières (S.E.E.F.), 166
Shone, Robert (Sir), 19, 20, 36, 38, 41, 46, 48
Strike, 123

Tariff wall: by Common Market countries, 8
Taxes: consumer, 10, 23, 26; relief, 109
Technical change: resistance to, 121
Technology Ministry, 62, 74, 76, 114
Thorneycroft, 3
Trade deficit, 157

Trade unions: 5, 9, 35, 43, 59, 80, 85–86, 113; 1959 Trades Union Congress, 13; and wages, 22, 36–40; responsibility of the staff of N.E.D.C., 37; partner in planning machinery, 38; end pay pause, 41; critical of export target, 47; incomes policy, 52; opposition to National Incomes Commission, 54, 94; French, 107, 123; bargaining, 124; movement, 127; productivity and wage increase, 130–32
Transport Ministry, 93
Treasury: 23, 30, 58, 81, 108, 114, 144, 148, 150; function, 26–27; move to end post budget approval, 28; reorganization, 29, 30, 31; policy decisions on public expenditure control, 32; relations with N.E.D.C., 36

Unemployment: 9, 22, 45, 66; compensation, 72, 89, 133, 150, 163

Wage policy: 16; increases in the private and public sectors, 24
Wilson, Harold, 18, 36, 62–63, 74, 126
Woodcock, George, 41, 85; on wage increase, 56